.... In music, any combination of notes will interact. Some notes have the propensity to create a stronger, more pleasing harmonic. Some create an interaction that could be called a harmonic but is unpleasant, a *discord*, and some combinations are so distant from each other that the interaction between them is too subtle for us to detect. As I have said, we do not choose to envision. We are doing it all the time. Every human being is always singing the three notes of its mind, body, and spirit. Sometimes the *notes* being sounded by an individual's mind, body and spirit are so distant from each other, so opposite, that their envisioned effect is impossible for the individual to detect. The interaction of these subtle forces still affects the world in a profound way. However, an act of the mind alone, or one which is in such discord with the simultaneous act of the body, or one with no coordination with spirit does not produce a strong harmonic and thus it does not become experienced by the individual. *Conscious Envisioning* is a function of mind, body and spirit in close and *beautiful* harmony. ....

The Art Of Conscious Envisioning

By

Patrick Munson M.D.

Copyright Reserved
1-15-2007

ISBN 978-0-6151-6031-3

Acknowledgements

When I began this book I was naive to the process and to how much help bringing the project to this point would require. I remain very thankful for the help of, Donna Burnette, without whose patience and thoughtful conversation and sharing I could not have learned enough about myself to write. And, to Nancy Stokes and her friend Ruth, who kindly consented to be a first readers, a task I would now not wish on any loving soul. Penny Corbett for tireless close reading and many friends for support and the example of their lives and experiences. I have had many teachers but Tom Brown Jr. remains the most influential among them save Stalking Wolf and Earth Mother herself.

Table Of Contents

Chapter One

The Path Toward Conscious Envisioning

Defining The Path 17
- Stages Of Change 24
- Concepts For Envisioning, Tier One 28
    - There Are No Rules 29
    - Method And Means 34
    - Compassionate Communication And Humility 28
    - A Power Beyond 41
    - Review Tier One 45
- Concepts For Envisioning, Tier Two 48
    - Understanding Harmonics 48
    - Becoming Conscious Of Our Harmonic 56
    - Breath Training 60
    - Pulse Timing 62
    - Mindful Meditation 64
    - Training The Breath-Observer Trigger 68
    - Review Tier Two 69
- First Envisioning, The Flow 70

Chapter Two

Whatever It Takes 77
- When Is An Illness An Illness? 80
- Accepting Our Diagnosis 93
- Bringing It Home 98
- Denial And Willingness 101

Chapter Three

Climbing The Pyramid 110
- Surrendering Value Judgment 101
- Knowing Clarity 124
- Purity 135
- God And Evolution 146
- Interlude: Why Bother? 148
- Climbing To The Top 155
  - Rigorous Honesty 155
  - Releasing Expectations 160
  - Shame And Denial, Purposeful Presence 161
  - The Posture Of Recovery, And Gratitude 163
- Summary 169

Chapter Four

Using Envisioning 174
- Paying Attention To Coincidence 174
- Upstream Energy 181
- Envisioning For Others 197
- Seeing The Soul 203
- Self And Carrying An Agenda 208
- Power 213
- Creative Mechanisms 221
- An Example of Envisioning for Self 228
- The Dynamics Of Need 231
- Expansion Of Self 240

Prologue

If it were possible to walk through each of your days knowing with certainty that each moment you come closer to experiencing the truth of your relationship with yourself and with the world around you, would you desire it? If this same process of awakening could allow you a physically healthy body, a joyous life, and the feeling that you are pursuing something of great intrinsic value, would you pursue it? If you had a choice between walking in the dark imagining there is light or actually walking toward the light, which way would you choose? This is the actual situation. This is the truth of our relationship with our physical lives. No matter if you are religious or not. No matter if you are young or old. No matter if you are currently healthy or ill. No matter if you are rich or poor. These are the choices presented by being in relationship with the physical realm. We all have the same choices. Each of us chooses in each moment consciously or unconsciously. The Art of Conscious Envisioning is the process of learning to choose more and more consciously.

Introduction

What Is Envisioning?

Envisioning is the act of pretending times twelve plus the magic of consciousness! We already live within the presence of unconscious envisioning every minute of our lives, yet we disregard its presence and its importance. With the art of conscious envisioning we are thinking about waking up to this simplicity now. But, waking up to simplicity can be more difficult than studying something complicated. The emotions stimulated and the feelings created can be more personal and the changes will come to our most basic and fundamental levels and they will be holistic.

I am 51 years old but most people estimate my age at 40. I have a cold every now and then but I haven't had to miss a day of work or be uncomfortable at work in fifteen years. About twelve years ago I fell twenty feet from a rock onto a tree and could have severely injured myself but I was lucky and have no residual effects. I injured my knee last year but it has healed. I am in good enough shape to sailboard in 20 knots of wind on vacation even though my exercise regimen includes at most thirty seconds each morning and two 7 minute workouts a week. I eat reasonably well but I am not fanatical. I am not saying that this is extraordinary but as a physician I am often asked, "What do you do, doc?" My answer is, "I study the Art of Conscious Envisioning."

Envisioning is the act of pretending times twelve plus magic. If you can imagine yourself as you wish to be, and then make that imagining more and more real until it is actually more real than what you previously considered to be real, you will have envisioned your new self. That new self doesn't immediately pop into existence but it is one step closer. Envisioning is a process that requires tools. The first tool is your mind. Coming to know your mind as a tool you use, but not as the location of your self is the first step. The next tool to learn is your body. There is great wisdom and experience encoded in the body, and envisioning requires access to that knowledge. The body is also a tool of the self, but it is not the whole self. Next, we must study awareness as a pure sense. Knowing your awareness as the function of self that defines your location within the entirety of possibility, but not more than that, opens a doorway that leads to the ability to make envisioning functional. Assembling the tools of envisioning brings us closer to knowing our full selves. We are not just a point of awareness or a body located at that point. We are not just our thoughts. We are all three, and much more. We are the connection to magic. The process of envisioning requires that we study uncommon subjects and find the willingness to let go old ideas while we examine our experience looking for the traces of that magic. At times it is unsettling. It must be for us to come into a new sense of our own being.

Understanding the process of Envisioning without knowing the tools may make it seem not just magical, but impossible, just as advanced computing and flying to the moon seemed impossible not too long ago. But once the tools to accomplish the tasks are at hand, the process becomes simply the act of using the tools. One of the advantages we have at this time in history is that we have all experienced personally, or witnessed through the news, events that people of centuries ago would have dismissed as impossible. We now accept that many accomplishments of humankind are possible even though we, as individuals, do not understand the steps, or tools, that make them possible. The process of envisioning is just the same. Envisioning is, in fact, a completely natural process. It has been my experience, in looking at my life and the lives around me, that envisioning is not unusual in anyway. It is, rather, what human beings are designed to do.

I was first exposed to the idea of envisioning through Tom Brown Jr's Tracking and Wilderness Awareness School (www.trackerschool.com). Tom's teachings are descended from the Apache. Tom Brown translated, refined and brought to the western mind the teachings of his mentor Stalking Wolf. Perhaps many Native Peoples utilized envisioning in their lives and cultures, but I feel the Apache elders advanced conscious envisioning to an art form.

Human beings typically learn by relating new concepts to understandings we already have. This can present a problem for those beginning their study of envisioning because the concepts of envisioning contradict many commonly held ideas and beliefs. Only new experience can settle this conflict. No amount of thinking can. The phrase I use, "in the end, only results count," refers to this. The results of new experience tell us whether the new idea or the old one is valid. In native cultures there was a tradition called 'The Empty Cup'. Before coming to the elder, healer or shaman, the questioner would prepare with the process of 'The Empty Cup'. Simply, the questioner would take time to put aside what they thought they knew. This would be done to prepare for the new knowledge so that no old ideas or structures of belief would compete with the new understanding. Once the new knowledge was heard and understood the person would then go out and examine their old understandings and see how they fit with the new information. In the light of experience, ideas that worked were reintegrated, and ideas that were now outdated or superceded were abandoned.

We are practiced at accepting things in our lives that we do not completely understand. How many of us actually understand a toaster? Not just the red wires but the timing mechanism, the electricity, heat by resistance; the whole thing? We are conditioned to live closely with things and events that we don't really understand. We accept this easily, especially if the object or process is something that we see as complicated. Once the complex process is accepted we maintain a peripheral awareness of it just accepting that we don't understand.

However, when the process is simple, so simple that it goes unnoticed, we can become entirely unconscious of it. This is essentially our relationship with envisioning.

No one can convince another to become aware of envisioning. Envisioning is an act of the heart. To discuss this in a book as I am attempting means that experiential concepts must be rendered into words and stories. These will always be incomplete and inexact; still, to write and read is valuable. Words like "knowing," "balance in mind body and spirit", the "pure moment of the present", and "pure experience in the moment of the present", will need to become real and exact within your own personal experience. These are the tools we discover within ourselves as we come to consciousness in our envisioning.

Right now these concepts may feel confusing, or like partly understood ideas that relate loosely to past experiences or to what you have read. Alternatively, they may seem like concepts you do understand and think you know everything about. Regardless, in order to learn something new our cups must be emptied for a time. Our concept of ourselves, as we currently understand ourselves, is valuable. All that we now know is not to be cast aside for all time, but to learn something truly new we first have to become empty. There will be a time for reintegration and for reconsideration of all that we thought we knew. We will value each detail and decide, after we have allowed ourselves to open to the new experience. Then we will know what is true for us and what may no longer be true. Nothing is lost, but often the secret that seems hidden is in plain view and we have simply forgotten it, placed something over it, or cast it aside.

The Art Of Conscious Envisioning

Chapter 1

The Path Toward Conscious Envisioning

Defining The Path

The first step on the path toward conscious envisioning is to recall the time of childhood when pretending came naturally. Some of us actually remember this time, others have forgotten, but all of us had in our early childhood, a time when pretending was our favorite pastime. At seven or six we did it with props such as model cars, airplanes or dolls. At five or four or three a stick could become whatever we wanted it to be. Before that, we pretended without any props at all. We all came from a time when pretending and being were intermingled. First pretending has to be remembered then it has to be refashioned into a tool suited to our adult selves.

I need to be clear about an essential division in 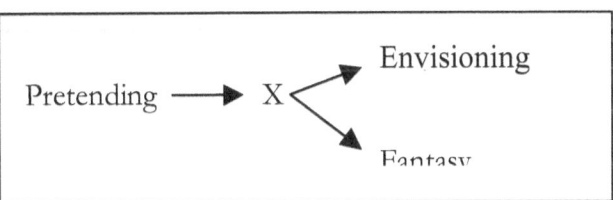 the adult relationship with pretending. Pretending delivers us to a branch in the trail. At this branch there is a differentiation between envisioning and fantasy. This distinction is the most important part of understanding envisioning. Envisioning is not fantasy. By definition fantasy is unreal. Envisioning is real, but what makes the difference? The quality of awareness at the point of the 'X' makes the difference. When awareness at the X is ordinary, the result is no more than wishful thinking or daydreaming, but when magical awareness occupies the 'X,' conscious envisioning becomes possible. Essentially, magical awareness is our conscious connection to the present moment. This is what actually makes results happen. I call it magic because, like the primitive looking at what he does not understand, the match, or the telephone, it seems like magic. Once awareness of the authentic moment of the present is attained in consciousness experience, we will understand the mechanism and it won't be magic anymore. Until then, there is nothing wrong with calling it magic.

This magic is the difference between dieting and becoming slim, between exercising and being strong, between hoping or fantasizing or wishing, and experiencing actual change. Envisioning acknowledges, and involves a power, or a presence beyond the self. The details of the conception of that power do not matter. The names used, the images evoked, the traditions or non-traditions involved *do not matter*. By definition, if you are asking for magic, it has to be something beyond your understanding. If you haven't had the experience of consciously creating your own reality then it is by definition, beyond you. This is the place to start. It is honest, real, and authentic. It is the only true place to start, at our not knowing. So, there is a question. Are you ready to expand your world beyond what you currently understand? Are you willing to surrender your experience to a power or presence beyond yourself? That is the essential question separating ordinary life from magical life. Many people, perhaps most people, aren't ready for it, and this lack of readiness manifests as arguments over the qualities or descriptions of power beyond, but these details are unknowable. It is not what you understand as power beyond that is in question. The question is, are you ready to surrender control of your experience in order to experience something entirely new?

When I make dinner I am the combiner of ingredients and within my control is the choice over the ingredients I add, how much of each, and when. I also control how I prepare it, hot, cold, room temp and when I serve it. In a sense I am arranger of the dinner. I have *created* none of it. My true relationship is that I am in a secondary position to the act of Creation. If I want an essentially new ingredient I would have to reach beyond my entire knowledge and experience of the world. I would have to involve something entirely beyond my understanding and experience. In order to *experience* something entirely new, I would have to consult with something, a power or presence, entirely beyond myself.[1]

In the beginning of my experience with Envisioning I didn't have the perspective to be aware of a relationship with any power beyond myself. My church experience as a youth had not given me a clear sense of any such relationship and as I have said I was not, and am not, good at having faith before experience. About 1991, two years into my exposure to envisioning through Tom Brown's school, I went camping alone. I had walked only an hour from my car and I knew that in need I could get back to it in the dark. Planning to practice my survival skills I didn't bring any equipment with me except my wool blanket and a knife. It was a beautiful afternoon and I was in an area where Nature was spectacular. Knowing I was only spending one night I planned and built a shelter that was mostly lean-to style with a mattress of cattail. It was evening before I got around to making my fire.

I carved a bow drill in the evening light watching the sunset and feeling a wind beginning to kick up. A bow drill is a primitive fire-making apparatus that I had practiced with for more than a year. I felt confident that I could make a fire.

---

[1] I will shorten this to just 'Power' because as time goes on in your experience of envisioning you come to understand that in this realm power - the ability to affect, and presence - the ability to be are the same.

The wind was a little worrying as it was beginning to carry an edge of cold. Back at my shelter I prepared the fire area and set my kindling ready to receive the flame. It was time to stroke up the drill to produce a coal that I would blow into flame. Darkness was moving in and I was hungry after the effort of the walk, shelter building and carving. I knew that though I could make fire in daylight making it in dark would be a challenge. I didn't have a flashlight and I needed the fire to cook the rice I had brought for dinner.

Primitive fire making is one of the magical interfaces in the study of Nature. Like animal tracking, it brings together a physical act with a cognitive skill, but ultimately it depends on spiritual connection. I tried hard in my first attempts at making a coal. It took what strength I had remaining. By the end I was sweating in wind that was now finding itself into the cul-de-sac I had chosen for my shelter. My arm was sore. I had produced a lot of smoke. I had attempted to turn the results over to spirit. But, all I had were shaking muscles, a warm stick and no fire. I decided I had to rest even though I knew it would require the remaining light. I went back out to the edge of the forest where I had carved the drill and sat down to watch the last pink rays turn to purple and then be gone.

It was full dark. I found my shelter not by seeing it but by feel. I found the drill, tinder, lubricating plants, and bow where I had readied them. This time I knew I had only one effort and since I couldn't see the quality of the smoke, it was all going to have to be by feel. When making fire with a bow drill apparatus, the goal is to make dust that is hot enough to nurture into a glowing coal with small careful breaths. I had been successful at making fire a hundred times and once or twice even in the dark, but never cold, tired, or in actual need. To blow the coal one watches the quality of smoke and judges how much air to use. In the dark it has to be done by feel or smell. I did my best, I worked at it much longer than usual; until no warmth was left.

Resigned to giving up and walking back to my car, as it was now too cold to stay in the shelter I had prepared without a fire, I stood up and wandered to the edge of my little camp. I asked myself what I had done wrong, but I knew that I had done my best. At that time I had no relationship with the magic of envisioning. My study so far had been at the physical level of tracking and survival. As I went back to gather my knife and blanket, I saw, in the pitch black by the fire area, a small red dot glowing. There were chills running down my neck as I knelt down and saw that there in the kindling was a healthy coal. In a few minutes I had blown it into flame and had a roaring fire going. I stayed up late into the night grateful for that fire. I knew it had been a gift to me. I did not understand where it had come from but it was cooking my food and keeping me warm and in good company.

This was one of my first experiences with knowing that a power beyond myself is at work in my life. I saw that night's fire as a gift from the Earth to me. I have carried that gift ever since and it has taught me nearly every day. I had been the combiner of the ingredients for the fire. I did my part in being ready, including coming to fully understand my need. The sensation of experiencing magic is what I learned that night. Any number of physical excuses came readily to my mind. Had I not been ready I could easily have ignored the experience. I could have thought myself just lucky, and if I had absolutely nothing would have changed in my life.

Are you ready to wake up? I believe that envisioning is not a new thing. I believe that for people who live close to the Earth and close to their needs it is a natural process. As I have said, the Apache were masters. There are many groups and cultures throughout human experience that have been masters of envisioning (Spaulding, "The Lives and Teachings of the Masters of the Far East"). Envisioning has not been lost. It cannot be lost. Regardless of how distant you may personally feel from things of the spirit, just as you did not create the world, or create yourself, you did not design the mechanism of existence. No matter how you currently conceive of it, scientifically, religiously, new-age-y, or in some individual version, the essential mechanism of being is beyond our human understanding and control at this moment in history. It is beyond our understanding, but it is not beyond our experiencing. Envisioning is hidden in its simplicity. We *unconsciously understand* it and this is expressed as experience, but we do not *consciously understand* it because we do not apply our consciousness to this understanding. Instead, we experience it in every moment and hold it so close to us that we are unaware of it. In this way we are in contact with the very mechanism of existence and its method of manifestation. It is not a question of doing it or not doing it. We have no real choice in the matter of envisioning, except as to whether or not we become conscious of it. Thus the 'study' of the *art* of envisioning is the process of coming to consciousness of our envisioning. The question, "are you ready to wake up," does not ask if you are ready to envision, it asks "are you ready to become consciously aware of your envisioning."

It is a big thing, to become conscious. There are many ramifications. Among them are guilt, fear, apathy, responsibility, motive, individuality, relationship with the collective, the depth of self, health and healing, consequence, cause and effect, love, anger, duration, appearance, acceptance, courage…. The meaning of all these concepts will shift. For a time it will produce a sensation of uncertainty. This uncertainty may evoke fear; the resistance to feeling fear may produce anger and a pushing away, or, it may produce shame and the feeling that one is not good enough or smart enough to understand. All these are natural human reactions to waking up. No one can force another to wake up or to be ready. Within each individual, it is possible that being ready is not an act of will, but one of recognition. Sometimes we may experience moments when we would like to be ready but actually we just aren't. Perhaps there is some unconscious experience that still needs to be in place. In the words of a friend of mine, 'They just needed to do it one more time' (Joe). There is no judgment, nothing to be looked down upon. An individual is not better than or worse than another depending upon whether he or she is ready, because the ultimate ability we all have to awaken and become powerful is equal. We didn't create ourselves. We are not in charge. The great weight and effort of striving is not required and can be relinquished at any time. There is a time for each of us to awaken. So, asking, "are you ready?" is not a challenge. It is just a question.

How do you tell if you are ready now? It may seem like an impossible question. Yet, there is a simple way. An individual's readiness is proportional to their willingness to accept the concept that there are no meaningless coincidences. Are you ready to accept that there are no accidents, that everything happens for a reason even if we do not understand it? This is the initial clue that there is something acting in our experience that is beyond our current understanding. As long as it is possible for you to go through your moments ignoring the events around you, or assigning them only to random forces that have nothing to do with you, the mystery of envisioning will remain hidden. As soon as the question appears; "what is the meaning of this event?" or "what does this have to teach me?" you are ready. Usually, once the door opens it never closes solidly again.

You may prefer to think that "sometimes a cigar is just a cigar" as Freud put it. You may be more comfortable thinking that the world is mostly unaware of you and that most of the events surrounding you just happen. You may enjoy examining some of these events to see what you might learn from them thinking that whatever meaning you find is arbitrary, applied by you, and not intrinsic to the event itself. This will help to maintain the notion that there may be meaning to the world or there may not; coincidence abounds and has no real significance except that which you assign. In this way you may maintain, for a while longer, a comfortable distance from awakening. These ideas can easily fill your cup of knowledge and prevent new knowledge from entering. For a while longer it may be more comfortable than considering that things *never* just happen, that it all makes sense in some very large and very intimate way.

In many ways having a book speak directly to you is uncomfortable. We prefer our distance. I do too, but I have learned that this is not an effective way to learn about conscious envisioning. Rather, it is what continues to suppress my awareness of envisioning into my unconscious. Remember, that when Freud made his statement, the very notion of the unconscious mind was new. Now, we accept it naturally. What is new, now, is the notion we might bring the light of full awareness into every corner of human experience and know the meaning and personal relevance of everything. In effect, the universe of experience would change and 'a cigar would never again be, just a cigar.'

Stages Of Change

Psychologists have mapped out the stages of change: pre-contemplation, preparation, action and maintenance. I have added a little to make it fit envisioning but the concept that there are characteristic feelings and experiences that occur at each stage remains true.

1. *Unconscious Envisioning*

This stage may include the whole of a life. It is the most common place. It is characterized by a style of attention that remains focused on the physical level of existence. An individual at this stage may be moneyed or poor, successful by common definitions or not. As this phase begins to mature into the next there is often manifested a period of feeling driven, frantic, ultra busy, but with an unwillingness to develop priorities that include the deeper aspects of life. I see many people in this place. They are coming to the point of being able to look deeply into their lives but are still resisting. Relationships may fracture, addictions may develop, 'accidents' may occur, symptoms of all sorts develop and real disease can result. The feeling is one of desperation, which if not transcended, can lead to exhaustion, depression, chronic illness and even death. In this state envisioning is still occurring but it is entirely unconscious. These are the patients that ask their doctor, "do you think it could be stress?" It is the combination of the desire to awaken mixed evenly with the natural resistance to change. In the passage from completely unconscious life to awakened life this midpoint has to come sometime.

I am often reminded, while witnessing this phase, of the young child who resists sleep until it is impossible to resist any longer, and then literally falls over. That period of resistance can be torture for the parent, as the child refuses to sleep by ramping up movement, becoming uncooperative and regressing into old stubborn behaviors. Surrender is resisted to the last of available strength. But, in any case, the end of this transition comes. The resistance to awakening to conscious envisioning can be experienced as, work-a-holism, panic, depression, hypertension, heart attack, inflammatory bowel disease, etcetera, etcetera. If the soul comes to believe that the ego has learned, or remembered, all it can in this life but still will not let go, then the soul may bring about the end of this life. but if this mechanism of resistance and its symptoms can be recognized as such, resistance to movement to the next phase, then this transition can be accepted naturally and the symptoms averted. We easily accept phases of our development during childhood. When potty training is excessively resisted we understand that abdominal cramping can be a symptom. This transition is a phase of our adulthood. It can be a normal healthy, enjoyable phase of our growing. Then we can realize that our symptoms even unto death may simply be insistent triggers helping us to move on to our next phase.

2. *Pre-contemplation*

This is the stage where you hear the phrase, *that was weird*, referring to a coincidence that stood out in consciousness as too unlikely to have absolutely no significance. Often, the pull of remaining unconscious is still strong enough to keep the individual from looking for the hidden meaning in the coincidence. The label *weird* suffices to quell the superficial curiosity, but the hunger for awakening is still strong enough to keep the awareness of coincidence strong and alluring. In this phase accidents become occurrences of interest and it starts to become clearer that the motivations of discomfort, ill circumstances, and diagnosable illness occur in inverse proportion to the acceptance of non-coincidence. This can be a frustrating phase because there has been no well-defined, commonly known method for the study of the art of conscious envisioning in our society. The pre-contemplative individual knows there is more going on, but doesn't know what to do about it. It is likely that, if you are still reading this, you are in this phase.

3. Action

In this phase there is full acceptance of the fact that there are no meaningless coincidences. This is where the Apache had the advantage. Their culture accepted and nurtured this phase implicitly, and this acceptance vastly shortened the two preceding phases. This is the phase of the work we are talking about in this book. The work is detailed. There are specific steps that produce specific results. As with any art we each must approach the art of conscious envisioning as individuals, but there are certain elements of the experience, which are common to us all. Each of us, including myself, is on the same journey. Reading, consulting experts, is important, but remember that your specific program, the one individual to you, must be constructed individually. This is your journey. What can be written is a general description of the path. The specific content, and, especially, the specific meaning will relate to you as a unique individual.

4. Maintenance

Though this is a stated phase in the understanding of change it is less applicable to envisioning because conscious envisioning is an *art*. No artist is ever truly finished exploring, growing or expanding. When the process stops the artist disappears. So there may be a phase of maturity when envisioning has become a known, active, and developed part of your life, but it will continue to grow. Your understanding of it will continue to deepen and, if you choose, you will always be engaged in the process.

5. *Relapse and Recovery*

Inevitably each of us will relapse into deterministic, Newtonian, cause and effect thinking. For me this is a daily occurrence. Envisioning asks only for balanced functioning in mind, body and spirit, which includes an awareness of our relationship to power beyond self. I am constantly reminding myself of my choices to perceive possibilities rather than absolutes. There are times when I struggle for days or weeks before I remember the authentic journey of my deeper self. I believe this is human. To be otherwise is perhaps to become enlightened, but so far my journey has been to explore the path, to enjoy the journey, and to experience my life with others who are journeying also.

Concepts For Envisioning, Tier One

There are two levels of concepts that are needed in our initial approach to envisioning. I call these tier one and tier two. The difference between the two tiers is that the first tier includes simply information. It is only important to know about it and to consider it. It isn't even important to believe or accept the information as true at first. The experience of conscious envisioning will prove out the first tier concepts in time. The second tier, however, includes experiential concepts which must be experienced in order to be understood. There is more work here but this is where the experience of conscious envisioning is hidden.

There Are No Rules

Although the actual description of envisioning is extremely simple, in order to actually make it work, that is, to actually create change in your life, there are tools that are essential to understand and to come to use naturally. At this early stage these can be thought of as the strategy for conscious envisioning or as ingredients or elements of the path, but it is important not to think of them as rules. A *rule* is authoritative in nature. With envisioning there are no outside authorities. Thus, there are no *rules*. You may imagine anything you can conceive of.[2] You may pretend anything! But, bringing these imaginings to manifestation in your life requires a strategy or a combining of essential ingredients. The process of envisioning presents choices that come to bear on the power of your envisioning or its ability to actually create change. Eventually the process transcends words like *strategy*, *elements* or *ingredients*. It has already transcended *rules*.

It is important to remember always that envisioning is not something that we have to learn *how* to do. Each of us is doing it, unconsciously, already. In every moment we are fulfilling our nature. For this reason it is good to start with the understanding that Envisioning is not something that it is possible to 'try' to do. While we will study it, and analyze it in some detail, we will see that the actual act of conscious envisioning is one of pure awareness accepted as an act of doing. If you 'try to do' something, by definition you are

---

[2] There is nothing in envisioning that is in conflict with religion. During the time of the inquisition there was the notion that thoughts were to be censored. In the end, I think it can be honestly be said that this notion was a mistake. Religions of the present do not attempt to censor thoughts. They do often judge them but this judgment then becomes a choice. At this level of choosing to accept the judgment *you* are choosing the dictate of an outside authority. The primary choice is still yours.

blocking the knowledge that you are already, unconsciously, doing it.

The elements of Envisioning that we are going to go over are like the petals on a flower. The colors of the petals and their relationship will attract your attention to the center as actual flower petals attract bees. Just by reading about these ideas you will take a step toward your understanding of envisioning. For the ideas in this section only exposure is needed. You do not have to believe the ideas or be convinced. We have built up many layers of camouflage between ourselves and the world. As envisioning becomes conscious these layers will peel away naturally.

There are phases in the process of becoming conscious where it is useful to focus conscious attention on envisioning but only within the context of understanding that it is already happening. It is a little like trying to slip a word or two into a conversation with a companion who is constantly talking. Your word, your conscious intention, must be *slipped* into the conversation. If it is to be effective, it must fit in, or even add to the flow so that the listener, your unconscious in the case of envisioning, becomes interested and willing to give you another moment of attention. Because we are unconsciously envisioning every moment of our lives we have a 'full slate' going at all times. The project of consciously affecting this continuous stream of unconscious envisioning is subtle. When we are 'trying' we are moored on the surface of things and this is much too superficial to cause real change.

I remember a time when my son was six years old. He had invited several friends over to play. He had been planning all the things he wanted to do with his friends, days before. I was watching the group of them playing. After they had been jumping for a while on the trampoline I observed my son, at first suggesting and then nearly ordering them to stop jumping, and move on to the next activity. He was becoming angry and was distancing himself physically from the others who were still jumping, so I called him over. I could see that he was upset so I motioned for him to sit next to me. After a minute of sitting watching his friends I asked him what was going on. He rapidly explained to me that he wanted them to stop jumping and switch to playing with this throwing toy he had. "Looks like they are having fun jumping on the tramp," I said. He didn't look at me but replied, 'Yea, but they are going to get bored in a few minutes and if they switch now they won't get bored."

I was impressed. He wasn't just attempting to exert control. He had sensed a not so desirable future event, and correctly or not, he was acting to change that future to one he thought would be better for all. I'm his dad. I was willing to give him the benefit of the doubt. So, I suggested that sometimes a good leader simply went and did what he wanted others to do. If it looked good to them perhaps they would join in. He popped off from beside me and began throwing the toy and in about two minutes the kids had gradually been attracted over. To me, it looked like he had been correct.

This story is not really an example of Envisioning but I'm telling it to show the psychology of interacting with systems that are already occupied. Jacob attracted the other kids away from the trampoline and toward what he was doing. He had tried to force them and it didn't work, but shifting his own attention attracted theirs. It is just the same with Envisioning; our unconscious mind body spirit interaction is busily envisioning all the time; to insert something consciously, we will have to attract its attention.

In a one-sided conversation, if what you want to say is not something the other person is ready to hear, they are likely to tune you out. What is needed is something that catches their interest without fueling their anger, shame or fear. It has to have some relevance, it has to be of some interest, and it has to fit in without judging, instructing, or otherwise criticizing. The same is true of envisioning except the person you are affecting is yourself, your unconscious self. The same concepts apply. If what you are attempting to consciously envision angers, shames, embarrasses, scares, or otherwise dis-comforts your unconscious self, it is likely to deny you its attention and thus prevent your conscious attempt to envision. It is possible that this is the mechanism of *wishful* thinking. If I *try* to envision that I possess a Ferrari, it embarrasses me. So the result is no Ferrari, just the wish for one. You cannot stop the process of envisioning. We can only change our connection to it. If not we will just keep on envisioning the same old stuff.

What happened in the example of my son is that he found an effective way to communicate with his friends. His friends had not been actively resisting him. They were simply keeping on doing what they had been doing. Effective communication broke that inertia so the something new could slip in.

The key to effective conscious envisioning is, also, effective communication. For envisioning, the goal of this communication is to open a wide conduit between your conscious self and your unconscious self, and to include a power beyond yourself. This communication can be modeled, practiced, and perfected with other people and then applied to your internal environment. Others who are also studying the art of conscious envisioning will be especially helpful, but any others will do. This communication must be honest and humble. The combination of these attributes of communication can be labeled *compassionate communication*. Thus, the study of compassionate communication is central to the art of conscious envisioning. To begin the effort does not require that you are an expert, just that you are aware of and willing to pursue what you need. There will be more on compassionate communication later.

It is common, in my personal experience, to meet individuals who have been brought to a willingness to study the envisioning by some aspect of their health. But, while likely that some specific symptom that may awaken your interest it is way too close to you to be your first conscious envisioning project. This is because your health is a sensitive subject. Illness is the result of many years of unconscious envisioning. Often, the illness's underlying content is related to many of the important people and events in your life. There may be many layers of judgments and resentments hosting this unconscious envisioning and all of them must be brought to awareness before things can really change. With illness this is usually the case. Also, changes in our envisioned self are the most difficult. It requires the most humility, honesty and the cleanest communication with power beyond. After all, if you could understand it from your ordinary level of consciousness, trying would work, and you could just do it directly! This is where envisioning seems the most like magic. You are so close to all the issues because they are what create the *you* that you know. There is an old saying: It is hardest to see the wart on your own nose! This is why readiness is measured by willingness to give attention to coincidence. Coincidence is first seen as outside of the self and, it is through coincidences that the first results of your conscious envisioning will appear. It is by accepting that these are important events, not random accidents, that you will become aware that a change in you is occurring.

At first, accepting the risks involved in compassionate communication, and placing our imagination at the feet of a power beyond ourselves, feels strange, awkward and unlikely. Becoming honest with oneself is much easier to do regarding aspects of your life that are not central to your highest emotions or most difficult experiences, such as illness. Later, when some experience is gained, the elements involved in your health will make their way into your envisioning naturally and without effort.

Method And Means

The practice of envisioning will both produce change and let us know what our blocks are. It will help us grow, and it will let us know where our next most efficient growth area is. All it takes is the courage to be honest with ourselves, a willingness to communicate honestly and an understanding of humility. In twenty-five years of emergency medicine I have had ample opportunity to test the relationship between accepting the norm, that which we all unconsciously envision, and what I might envision on my own.

Once, in the emergency department, about eight years ago, I was treating a woman who had new onset atrial fibrillation. This is an abnormality of the heart in which the beat becomes irregular and often quite fast. Just the fast beating will make most people feel a little anxious, but she was very anxious and frankly afraid despite my reassurances. I began treating her with the usual medications, but nothing was working. I kept visiting her room each time expecting to find the situation improving, but it wasn't. Each time I left I attempted to envision her pulse slowing if not returning to normal. About the fifth attempt I realized that although I thought I was envisioning her improving, I was actually hanging on to control, and refusing to let the magic enter. I was in my ER doctor mode where I felt I had to be in control of everything. This is to say, I was conforming to the collective envisioning of what was my role. As soon as I let go of this control allowing the envisioning to flow through that which I cannot understand, her rhythm popped back to normal. Perhaps, it was a temporal coincidence. I had, after all, given her all the appropriate medications and these rhythms are known to pop back to normal spontaneously. But, I had the experience of feeling the envisioning flow inside me. The feeling of the change taking place in me, in her, and in the whole of the universe that represented her heart rhythm returning to normal, and the synchronicity of the event of her actual heart rhythm changing, was enough to make me pay attention. It felt like the magic moving. I have come to know that feeling. I have come to be able to recognize, sometimes, when I am blocking it by conforming to the unconscious envisioning of the collective. When I do, I welcome my individuality and the letting go.

Thus it was by my using the method of conscious envisioning that I came to awareness of the feeling of the magic moving, and it was by knowing that feeling, that I came to know when I was blocking myself. This is what I mean by both *method* and *means*.

Compassionate Communication And Humility

I have mentioned humility. This is a concept that holds difficulty for me and yet it is an essential element in compassionate communication with self and with others. Humility is needed in the study of conscious envisioning because, in the beginning, we come to recognize that many of our creations are not what we desire. As our awareness grows we need compassion for ourselves, or denial will overcome our new awareness and envisioning will be pushed into unconsciousness again.

Recently, I came across the most functional way of thinking of humility I have found. It is in David Hawkins' "The Eye of the I." Paraphrased, he says, "Humility is the recognition that all perception is approximate." I like this definition because it is removed from all considerations of hierarchy. From this definition comes simply the knowledge that we never truly understand each other. As individuals we never truly see the totality of our own envisioning or that of others. Whenever we think we 'know what is going on' we should remember that our point of view is only partial. Being humble, we can always look at the world around us in wonder knowing there is mystery and possibility everywhere. With humility we can hold compassion for everyone, including ourselves. Every event we witness with humility contains mystery because we know that all we think we understand is incomplete. Thus a coincidence becomes even more fascinating as we wonder what it might truly mean.

In the language of Tom Brown Jr's teachings, this is the lesson of the center skull. Tom relates this lesson through telling a story about himself and his friend, when they were young. They had gotten in a fight over the exact description of an event. They had been stalking a huge rabbit when an Owl suddenly took it right in front of them. Each boy was amazed that they had witnessed such an event, but also completely seduced by his own perception of what happened.

> Grandfather Stalking Wolf, Tom's Apache elder, broke up their fight and made them sit down facing each other with a skull between them. (Somehow knowing the boys had come to this lesson Grandfather happened to have a skull with him. He was like that.) He asked each of them to describe the skull in great detail. Of course, their descriptions differed by their respective points of view. The understanding dawned on the two boys that they could never actually witness the same event because they could never occupy exactly the same place at the same time. Thus our experience is entirely individual and always partial to the whole.

I learned this lesson years ago from Tom Brown Jr. but I never thought of it in connection with humility until reading Hawkins. Accepting that I can only know an approximation of the truth helps me to leave room for compassion. Compassion is the understanding that regardless of what I think or feel there must be a consideration that there is more to be understood. If I see someone that seems, to me, to be suffering, or doing wrong, in humility I must consider what it looks like from that person's point of view. When I feel that I am *right* and begin to push my agenda on others I must remember that others might not see it as I do. But, most importantly, this definition of humility helps me to leave room for the magic. Even though I feel certain at times, in knowing deeply that I see only part of the truth, there is still mystery. This allows room for the magic to occur. Just holding humility evokes the pathway of envisioning because it turns the actual truth over to a power beyond self.

Many modern philosophers have postulated that the universe is really designed to be a very large experience-manifesting machine. The template is inside us and the projection that appears outside us is what we call experience.

Depak Chopra talks of the 'field of infinite potentiality. ' In many religions there is the notion of 'ask and you shall receive.' In Tom Brown's teaching of the Apache Way there is the understanding of Spirit First. This is the way I hold this concept most easily. I am a pretty basic person. What it means to me is that 'things' whether they are emotions, events, or physical objects, exist in spirit first. They are then brought into the physical realm through envisioning and wind up as thoughts, or feelings, desires, plans, or experiences. For a period of time the holding of the idea of spirit first was useful to me. Eventually though, this also becomes just a construct of perspective. It is only because we are looking from the point of view of physical life that we must use the notions of first and second, before and after, primary and secondary, but that is for later. At this point spirit first (temporal) is useful. Spirit first teaches us that envisioning reaches toward spirit and then allows the mechanism of the universe to do its work.

Once while I was reading the book 'A Course in Miracles' I took a trip to Colorado with a friend. I had just read a section where the voice referred to as Jesus said, "Don't worry about the details. Leave them to me. What seems to be the past and the future to you, is not a barrier to me." Further, the voice added, "If you don't believe me give it a try. See what happens." I had just read this section on the plane before I met my friend and so as we were driving west from Denver I was telling him about it. I had taken up the challenge to give it a try, I told him.

About that time we had to pull off to get gas. We were just at the foot of the climb up to Loveland pass and the great divide. While we were paying the cashier she volunteered that she had just heard that the pass was closed by ice and snow. She said that the officers who told her had gone next door to the bar for dinner and that we could go over there and wait. It would be better than being caught on the road and the officers could tell us when would be a good time to continue on up.

All this seemed remarkably convenient to me and was enough evidence of small miracles, but when we went next door something entirely different happened. As we rounded the turn in the doorway to the bar the officers were there all right, but also there was a bartender. She had long wavy light brown hair and a magnificently gorgeous face. She was wearing a tight blouse and as I approached the bar I could see a short skirt and fabulous legs. At that time such a person was terrifying to me and I immediately anticipated being uncomfortable. However, just then, I recalled the statement. "Don't worry. Just leave it to me," and so somehow I did.

I sat down and she came over to ask what we wanted. "A Coke," I said, without the slightest debate about what she might think about me, a forty-something man asking for a Coke in a bar. She smiled, took my friend's order, made natural eye contact, and went about her job. We made conversation occasionally over the course of forty minutes or so and I felt comfortable. It is a small thing perhaps to individuals for whom this hasn't been a lifelong problem, but for me it had been the source of many embarrassing moments.

The officers asked if we were waiting for the pass and we told them we were. Their radio chimed. They told us the pass was open and we left. The drive over was uneventful except for numerous cars in the ditches. At that time I didn't know the process of envisioning. I was not studying the art. But, I know that the process that occurred was a process that I now think of as envisioning. I am not a devout Christian now any more than I was before, but I know that when I listened to the words in my head; "Leave it to me," I felt it in my whole being. It was not an act of mind alone or even of mind and body. It was of mind body and spirit acting together. I do occasionally feel the presence that I felt that night in those words. That presence doesn't seem to care about names or labels or traditions.

In that night more changed than just my fear of beautiful women. My memories of all the previous times changed and were not so shaming as they had been. Those memories were somehow more kind. I understood them as the reactions of a man learning rather than as a man who was timid and weak.

I have not had that paralyzing feeling with beautiful women since. I am quite sure that the relationship I now enjoy would not have formed if I had not changed. My partner has the kind of beauty that would have frightened and paralyzed me. I would have missed out on an experience I cherish greatly. In that one moment my entire universe was rearranged around what I wanted. It was not conscious envisioning but neither was it unconscious. It was in between. Often, that is the way of it. Do we really know what is best for us? Or is it better to dream and learn and grow with the magic?

Always, in envisioning, this is what we are doing. No matter if our desire forms because of the influence of something we read or whether we are specifically conscious of some of the meaning of our envisioning, we yearn toward a change in our personal reality and make our yearning so powerful, so rich with detail, that for us it approaches the real, and then we surrender it all. We humbly say that we do not know how this envisioned reality relates to the whole of reality. Within our humility we acknowledge that we cannot know. This act removes our ego's grip on our unconscious envisioning and our conformity to the collective. Thus unburdened our personal envisioning stands free in our own balance of mind, body and spirit. Now, our personal magic through our personal relationship with power beyond can remake the world for us.

A Power Beyond

It is fair to ask if envisioning is really just prayer. I think the answer depends on the context of the question. For the Apache, prayer was said to be 'in every step.' For some religions prayer might be held differently. We will take up the 'how to' for envisioning in the next section but suffice it to say that it is communication from your deepest, most aware self, with a power beyond yourself. Prayer as it is often recited can be a product of the mind alone. At times prayer is filled with passion which enters the realm of emotion and thus into the body, but envisioning is a balanced act of the mind, body and spirit acting in unison through what we will learn as 'a harmonic of awareness.' For myself the labels make no difference. If you choose to think of envisioning as a method of prayer, that is fine. If you wish to understand it as a cosmic mechanism, that will work too. But, envisioning becomes a way of life. This way of life brings more of what warms my heart and lights my eye. Prayer for me was something I learned to do in church. It was associated with rights and wrongs. Now, these are simply old ideas in my head. They make the word prayer less useful for me, but that is my personal experience only. It is important to know your own traps and habits. Learning this is part of the process of waking up. Sometimes, now, I can use the words "god" and "prayer" and mean something that comes from my heart and not my memory.

Having mentioned prayer it is useful to address another topic that many of us have learned in our childhoods. That is the concept of a vengeful power beyond or a *'Vengeful God.'* The concept that power beyond is interested in the concept of punishment and is capable of punitive action. This implies that you cannot choose your understanding of power beyond but that there is an absolute power that you must accept. This clearly has historical reference as people have believed in absolutes for a long time but, at this point in our exploration of envisioning let's just say that you may use any conception of power beyond in your envisioning process. If you can choose why would you choose one that is interested in punishment? I believe the idea of the vengeful god is an artifact of history, but it is still with us today. It may feel very real to you as part of your personal childhood history, or, it could simply be the collective weight of religious history. It doesn't really matter. The effect is the same; the notion of a vengeful, absolute, god creates a hesitation in your connection to power beyond.

I recently saw an expressway billboard that proclaimed "Prepare To Meet Thy God!" To me, this was an example of belief in a vengeful god. If you believe that somehow you have to prepare, be ready for, or in someway change in order to come into relationship with your personal version of power beyond, then, right now, your belief is that you cannot access that relationship, or, that if you contacted your power beyond before you are ready, you must fear that vengeance may be "meted out upon you." This belief, that right now you are not ready for, good enough for, or prepared for that relationship, separates you. "Vengeance is mine, saith the Lord."[3] All this

---

[3] The Bible, New Testament, Hebrews 10:30. My most remembered religious quotation though I have not traced it back to see if it was this way in the Sanskrit. I know that lots of folks have tried to write a way out from under this... often it seems that these were translation errors, or changes, that came along quite a bit later in the history of religion. And there is the notion that 'the Lord was reserving vengeance for himself, so as not to justify a person

will serve to sever your contact and thus your envisioning will not connect to the magic.

The idea of atonement is similar. Atonement is commonly defined as the making of reparation for a sin or a mistake. The purpose for atonement is to make you acceptable in the eyes of god... or some such. In Christian belief, atonement involves the belief that mankind was at one point so despicable that it required Christ to be crucified in order for the sins of mankind to be expunged. In the belief of one who accepts a vengeful god this common definition may fit; but in the belief of one who has found a loving god, it may have been that Christ having become so convinced that his god was loving that he was willing to play the role of expunging a guilt that was never real, never had any actual bearing on mankind's relationship with power beyond, but was blocking that connection. In this way atonement actually acceptance of *at-one-ment* or the recognition that power beyond and the "I" were/are/never can be, separate.

Regardless of how you choose to navigate these old traditions and beliefs, if you accept the notion of a vengeful version of power beyond, the surrendering of your self to your envisioning will be tainted by the notion of that power's judgment and it will go nowhere. The best evidence is always experience. Try envisioning with a vengeful power, a forgiving power, or no power beyond at all. Try envisioning with a universe infused with love and created to facilitate your envisioning, conscious and unconscious, and then try it with a universe that is a meaningless coincidence of physical properties. Check your own experience. I believe the results will be obvious.

---

taking vengeance et cetera, et cetera. As it is, though, it seems to create a pretty clear and very direct block to envisioning, perhaps to saving envisioning for a chosen few?

The other day I worked with a patient whom I have known for years. She is generally a very confident young woman with two children. She has owned and managed a successful day care business for a long time. Day care is a business that requires a high degree of personal integrity, problem-solving ability and flexibility. Recently the death of her mother and the addictive disease of her spouse have challenged her. Because of this she feels guilty and this guilt is absorbing all of her energy. Usually healthy, she has begun to suffer frequent small illnesses and is in danger of becoming depressed.

By understanding that those of us who fall in love with others who suffer from addictive disease do so, not by accident, but because we are learning our side of a lesson and, understanding that our side of the lesson is usually about our desire to control, it was easy to see that my patient's guilt originated from her feelings that she *should* have been able to prevent all these 'bad' things from happening. I had spoken with her before about her relationship to a power beyond herself so I knew she was familiar with the concept. I asked her if she believed in a vengeful power? She was a little taken aback and said no, she absolutely did not.

I asked, why then did she believe that she was guilty of negligence for not controlling all of the happenings around her? If the power she believed in was not vengeful how was it that it was all her fault? She began to see what I was getting at. By taking responsibility for events outside of ourselves we are usurping the place of that power. If our idea of power beyond ourselves is vengeful we might be held responsible. If we are willing to accept a forgiving power then there is no reason for our guilt. Recovery from this codependent side of addictive disease is just as significant as recovery from any other element of the disease.

Perhaps you and I will meet one day and debate the traditions and our ideas of 'God' and 'Power,' but in the process of envisioning only the results count. This is because only your own experience will convince you of the fact of envisioning. At this point I may have more conscious experience with envisioning than you do. Whenever I have witnessed an individual who is ready to see the significance of coincidence in their life but is still unable to sense their consciously envisioned experiences, invariably I find some version of a vengeful power. Paradoxically, usually all I have to do to break the hold of this pattern is to point out a few of his or her unconsciously envisioned events that have been proceeding right along as usual. By this time they are usually aware in some way of their conscious attempts and are influenced by the results. Once these results are seen, the illusion of the vengeful power loses status and dissolves.

Review Tier One Concepts

Let's take a moment and see where we are with our understanding of the process of envisioning. We have considered a number of aspects of envisioning. I think of these as the *first tier aspects*. That is, to become conscious of envisioning, awareness of these aspects is the first stepping-stone. They don't really come in any order. It is more like these concepts all have to be integrated. The awareness they engender together is the first step.

There are no rules to envisioning.

No outside authority exists to tell us that our envisioning will or will not be accepted. All events of the world are envisioned events, the *good* and the *bad*.

We are always envisioning.

Not because we decide to but because that is simply what we do. It is part of what we are. This is not something you have to believe because I say it. It is what you will come to notice if you accept that there are no meaningless coincidences and become willing to study the events of your life.

Compassionate communication is necessary for us to awaken.

This is because, if we are not compassionate with others and ourselves we will simply deny our awareness of envisioning each time it tries to surface.

Envisioning is both the method and the means.

In our attempts to become conscious of our envisioning, our blocks, resistances and denials will be shown to us, and through envisioning we will be given the opportunity to let them go.

To be humble is to understand that awareness is imperfect.

Accepting this understanding allows room for change. If all is known to us and understood totally, then our envisioning cannot evolve. Humility allows room for magic.

The universe is built to support your envisioning.

It divinely integrates, correlates and manifests each and all our envisionings into an understandable whole. If you are still living in a world with no power higher than your self, imagine that you are in charge of all the billions of individuals all combining coincidences similar to the ones you have been noticing. Like yours, each of their coincidences contains just the right next lesson for them as individuals. If you are ready to witness the coincidences in your life, and know that there is meaning in each of them, you must also know that you are not the only person in the game. If you are capable of managing such complexity you are truly a power higher than I. This is my definition of the divine: that which is capable of the complexity of a leaf, a snowstorm, and of me.

Envisioning is both a prayer and a way of life.

Any soul who comes to consciousness in envisioning sees the reality of life as a way of prayer. Envisioning is not a process of tradition; it is a method of being. It is our human way. To become conscious in envisioning is to become conscious of the magic in your relationship with power beyond yourself.

Belief in a vengeful god maintains denial of envisioning.

This is the result of perpetrating notions of vengeful gods. The experience of a relationship with a vengeful power is the fixation of the absolute. Not all is known, but the fear of vengeance is perfectly clear. This certainty blocks humility because the awareness of vengeance is felt as complete and it thereby it fills the space where the process of envisioning change would take place. It thus becomes a denial of the true nature of the relationship with power beyond, that of possibility. At best the vengeful god is a social tool for promoting behavior sanctioned by the collective.

Readiness to enter the study of envisioning is measured by the willingness to accept meaning in coincidence. The next step is to apply the first tier elements to your study of coincidence. Remember, if you are desirous but not quite ready to study envisioning there will be some conscious or unconscious fear of it, and you will take such a firm grip on your perceived reality that it will seem there are no coincidences around you anymore at all. You may remember a time when it seemed like there were some coincidences but now it will seem there are none. This state of denial requires a great deal energy and vigilance since you are envisioning against your own expanding awareness. Simply relax. The study of envisioning requires no effort at all. The statement, "all trying negates itself" is a favorite teaching of Tom Brown Jr. and many spiritual teachers. This is what it means. It is not that *not trying* is easier. Rather, not trying requires the student to apply no effort. The first step is that we must decrease our control over our envisioning so that something new can come into our awareness.[4]

Concepts For Envisioning, Tier Two

Understanding Harmonics

The first tier concepts are simpler than the second. On the first tier it doesn't really matter what you do with the concepts as long as they are in your awareness somewhere. You

---

[4] In 12 step language this is "Let Go and Let God". Often when a person comes into a 12 step program for the first time they are 'trying with all their might.' It feels very paradoxical when they see others who have been there awhile seem not to be expending any effort at all. Constantly, within addiction, there is the tendency to begin trying to control again. The slogan "Let Go and Let God" is to remind 12 'steppers' that this effort is misplaced. The effort to control is an attempt to usurp the power of that which is beyond us.

don't have to believe them. It is enough to know *about* them. During your process of becoming aware of your envisioning, the concepts of tier one will come back again and again. Each time, you will have a chance to adjust your relationship to them. Eventually, you will come to the relationship you personally need. Since there is no trying there is no work to be done.

> As you are sitting here, imagine that you are sitting on your couch at home. When your imagining has grown to the point where you *feel* more like you are at home, than here, you have reached envisioning.
>
> Tom Brown Jr.

In order to accomplish what Tom Brown Jr. is describing, all the elements of tier one must fall into the background and become simply part of the *place* of your pretending. We think of the act of pretending as a child's act. If you ask a child what they are doing and they say 'pretending' that is an acceptable answer. But if an adult were to respond similarly, you would feel that something was wrong. In adulthood pretending must either be abandoned (the usual decision) or elevated to something purposeful. This is because it is assumed that adults have a purpose involved in what they do. This is essentially true of the relationship between pretending and envisioning. Envisioning is pretending with an adult sense of purpose. The fact that that this purpose is held in connection with power beyond self and thus beyond the understanding of the ego allows the envisioned pretending to retain its humility and its fun.

In order to reach envisioning as Tom Brown Jr. is describing we have to understand that the word *feel* is the operative word. What we *feel* as real is a summation of our awareness through mind, body and spirit. That a pretended construct makes sense, is balanced and consistent in these three realms is our test for what is real. This balanced sense that tests reality is what I call a "harmonic" sense.

In music, a harmonic is the sound that several notes create when they are played at the same time. An Envisioned harmonic is what is produced by the harmonic of mind, body and spirit acting in awareness as one. In music, any combination of notes will interact. Some notes have the propensity to create a stronger, more pleasing harmonic. Some create an interaction that could be called a harmonic but is unpleasant, a *discord*, and some combinations are so distant from each other that the interaction between them is too subtle for us to detect. As I have said, we do not choose to envision. We are doing it all the time. Every human being is always singing the three notes of its mind, body, and spirit. Sometimes the *notes* being sounded by an individual's mind, body and spirit are so distant from each other, so opposite, that their envisioned effect is impossible for the individual to detect. The interaction of these subtle forces still affects the world in a profound way. However, an act of the mind alone, or one which is in such discord with the simultaneous act of the body, or one with no coordination with spirit does not produce a strong harmonic and thus it does not become experienced by the individual. *Conscious Envisioning* is a function of mind, body and spirit in close and *beautiful* harmony. Music can be uplifting and inspiring when its harmonies are beautiful. This appreciation of beauty can be said to occur because it awakens the connection to spirit within us. This is also true of envisioning. A harmonic of mind, body, and spirit that is beautiful awakens the connection to power beyond.

Tier Two is a *harmonic experience*. This means that the tier two concepts come together as harmonic elements of the envisioning process that must be *experientially* awakened in your mind, body and spirit. The action of tier two is to bring into conscious awareness the *experience* of harmonizing awareness of mind body and spirit: essentially, to do it consciously. We are familiar with the feeling of awareness in our minds; it feels like understanding. We know from experience that we may be mistaken, but we know the feeling of understanding within our minds. Awareness in our bodies most of us know only as movement and sensation. Yet, there is also great knowledge, memory, and experience locked in our bodies. This is the hidden awareness of the body. Experience in spirit is something the ancient cultures of the earth may have known better than we do today. It is a kind of awareness that can be sought particularly clearly in pure wilderness. Perhaps this is because there is less of the human element to cloud the voice of spirit there. Perhaps it is because the spirit of the earth is so strong in wilderness. In any case, the first steps toward gaining experience of awareness in spirit are straightforward.

Bringing the three aspects of experiential understanding into harmony is the launch pad for envisioning. The idea of pretending so clearly that the pretended reality becomes more real than the actual one is driven by learning to pretend *simultaneously* in all levels of mind, body and spirit. When this snaps into harmony that is when envisioning takes place. It is something many of the Apache had mastered. It made them very scary individuals to the uninitiated. This can be seen in the descriptions written by the first white men to meet them. "An ungodly stare" was a phrase used. I believe that might actually have been the look of a person who was living in a high level of mind body and spiritual harmony. It was very different from what the average European was used to.[5]

---

[5] The Apache were a people at war for three hundred years before the US Calvary even thought about fighting them. It was a common practice in what is now Northern Mexico and the Southwestern US for the Mexican mine owners to enslave natives for gold and silver mining. They preferred the Navaho and the Pueblo but occasionally they would ensnare an Apache. It was known at the time that if this happened the mine owners had to find the Apache and kill him or there would never be peace in the mine. There was no expectation that these slaves would ever see the light of day once captured, but still, all but the Apache could generally be cowed into their new existence. They thought of the Apache as 'devils' and actively hunted them whenever possible. Thus the campaign to eliminate the Apache predated US involvement

As an example, I once envisioned a change in my relationship with a person in my life with whom I was having some conflict. I knew clearly what I wanted in my mind. I wanted a clear flow of information and communication that worked as well for him as it did for me. In coming to honesty about this I realized that it was possible that I might hear things I didn't want to hear. With humility I acknowledged that I couldn't really know whether I would like it or not, but I had to be at least willing to hear his point of view. That was good, and had some power at psychological level, but it was not sufficient for envisioning.

Next I imagined what it would be like, hearing something I didn't want to hear, but not with my ears. I imagined the physical feeling of that interaction. How would my body feel if I were in that situation? I had to be ready and willing to feel the warmth of the friendship, the community of actually sharing. I also needed to be ready to feel the discomforts of shame if he told me something I didn't like about myself, or the hurt if he told me something about himself that was painful. I spent time imagining these sensations and combining them with the breathing we will discuss next to make them more and more real for me. This was good and powerful. The next time I saw him the residual of this mind body integration would be inside me and would pull our relationship in the direction I wanted, but it was still not envisioning.

---

and by the time the cavalry knew of them it is possible that, if there ever had been an average Apache, there were none left.

Describing the process of *imagining in spirit* is harder to write on a page. In the Apache tradition I took my mental and my physical imagining to my place of personal spiritual power. This is a place that I have built out of awareness over time. This building process is part of the means and method of the process of envisioning and is a natural result of pretending in the adult sense. It is something you can learn through experience alone but it can also be taught. This sort of pretending is like an exercise for our personal connection to power beyond.

We are spiritual beings. Of this I am clear. I am also clear that so much has been 'written' about spiritual experience that its essence is often clouded. What I know is that spiritual experience is *experience*. As such its essence will never fit into words. Spiritual experience is not a sub-vocalization in your mind. Sub-vocalization is ok and I'm not saying that such requests are invalid as a form of asking for help, but I do want to say that envisioning requires actual spiritual experience that you feel and know as such. Admittedly, this is the magic. If we understood it totally it wouldn't be magic and envisioning would be mechanical which clearly it is not. Much of the rest of this book is devoted to understanding this step of the envisioning process, the step of imagining in spirit.

In finally realized envisioning it is all done as one movement, one step but for now we will still break it down to its components. Like any skill our goal is the final fluid accomplishment but we can only get there by practicing each step individually until they come together within us.

- I combine
    - My mentally imagined relationship and my discovery that it may contain elements that I must learn from,
    - My physically imagined experience of being in that relationship; and
    - My spiritual experience of having the envisioning become my reality
- And then I hold that for a moment like a held breath and know that I am sounding a note into the universe: my note.
- And then
    - I release all thought, attention and concern about this process, the actual shape of my relationship, the effects of this relationship on others and myself.
    - I surrender all traces of effort in this direction,
- And most importantly,
    - I humbly remember that there is much more going on here than I perceive or understand.
- I rest in a feeling of gratitude and awe, not that I will manifest my wishes, but that the universe is such an amazing place within which to be.
- Then, I go back to being me as best I can. I observe the coincidences in my life and when I happen to come upon my friend I hardly remember that I had envisioned anything between us. Retrospectively, I notice that our conversation was comfortable and warm and that *coincidentally* he looked me directly in the eye and he told me something from his heart. It was the most natural thing and it was exactly what I needed, exactly what I had envisioned, plus magic.

As we have talked over the years since, I have come to know that there were many events and struggles and much learning that brought us to that moment. My envisioning was only a small part of the whole. The universe is grand and complex beyond our imaging but it does require that we each do our part. The whole is a sum of all its parts and of the magic. Our part is being added, consciously or un-consciously in every moment. It is built out of our unconscious fears, and denials, or from our courage and expanding awareness. *How* we speak our part into the whole is our decision.

Thus, the experience of envisioning involves the building up a harmonic experience in mind, body and spirit. Because the envisioning doesn't really exist independent of the experiential-harmonic, learning it is fundamentally different than learning other subjects. It is more similar to walking a trail; you are often in deep woods and cannot see very far, but occasionally a vista opens up unexpectedly and your breath is taken away by what has emerged in front of you.

In our culture lessons of the physical world are often presented in a linear fashion. That is, usually you are taught fact '1' that leads to fact '2' and gradually you come to an understanding. Material objects are often built by putting part 'A' onto part 'B' and gradually the object takes shape. Envisioning is different in both cases. The active principle is the harmonic of mind, body and spirit working as one in relationship with power beyond. It is the focused harmonic that *attracts*, not creates, the magic. The moment of the actual envisioning is hidden within the magic (in the relationship with power beyond) until we are willing to see it. It is our awareness, conscious or unconscious, that gives the opportunity for this magic to be present in the world. We do not do this by choice, or by an act of trying. We do it because it is our function. To walk the path toward *conscious* envisioning is to begin to add our gift of consciousness to the act of envisioning.

Becoming Conscious of our Harmonic

So, envisioning is built up as a harmonic of awareness. To study it, to become more conscious of it, we must study the harmonics of awareness. In my example, because I am limited by the linear nature of writing and communication, I presented my story as if I were performing step one, step two and so on. But, in reality, the notes of awareness in my mind body and spirit come together simultaneously. As in music, a 'harmonic,' is the sound that several notes make when they are played at the same time. It is not the notes themselves but the interaction of the notes. An envisioned harmonic is what is produced by the harmonic of mind, body and spirit acting as one. The presence of this harmonic opens the connection to power beyond and allows magic to enter the world.

In ordinary awareness, the level of the envisioning harmony is very sub-conscious. At ordinary levels of awareness our conscious minds and conscious bodies are expressing different messages at the same time and usually our spirit is ignored entirely. But, deep in our unconscious there is a level where we are always at harmony. No matter where this harmony exists, conscious or unconscious, this is the level of our *actual* envisioning because it is this level where we are expressing envisioning harmony and are in communion with power beyond. *Harmony*, as regards envisioning, does not mean, good or bad, desirable or noxious. It means the level at which our minds, bodies, and spirits are experiencing and expressing a close harmonic tone and where we are thus communicating with power beyond. For most of humankind this envisioning remains very basic and is driven more by fear than decision.

Most people lead lives *running from* rather than *moving toward*. That we may choose to come into conscious awareness of our harmonic is a gift of our nature. This is the central crux in the argument as to the existence of free will. During any time of unconscious envisioning, the experience is one where free will seems not to exist. By coming to consciousness of envisioning we may come into conscious ownership of what we have been all along. We may then choose to attract, or to produce in our lives, that which we consciously desire. This brings the gift of our personal free will into the world. It is the gift of who we actually are expressed in communion with power beyond through conscious envisioning.

For some of you reading this, it may seem like taking control where it may be better to *let natural processes be*. But, in the language of envisioning, you now understand that it is not a question of natural or un-natural, of exerting control or not, it is a question of coming to consciousness or of remaining unconscious. You might feel that you, or others, are not *responsible enough* or *mature enough* and, certainly in our world today, the issue of control over others is difficult at best. However, envisioning is our birthright. We do it in relationship to the physical realm because we were born. We cannot choose it or not choose it. We can only choose our level of awareness of it. Unlike wrenches and screwdrivers envisioning is a tool given to us, not created by us. We *do* it but we *do not* own it. This is the beauty of the harmonic. Spirit, in equal balance, is the governing force. Since consciousness in spirit is required for conscious envisioning, it is *impossible* to consciously envision something that goes against the intent of spirit.

Thus, we are back to the vengeful god question. Those who truly do believe in vengeful gods just don't seem to be able to consciously envision. Instead, they most often resort to force. The play of force in the world is reported daily in the news but compared to the effects of envisioning it is of a different order of magnitude. The effects of envisioning are less likely to make the front pages because of their subtlety. They are most likely to be anonymous. To me, this shows clearly their strength.

Comparing the effect on the world of Saddam Hussein to the effect of Gandhi or the effect of Hitler to Jesus shows the difference. And these are not anonymous effects of envisioning. Had it been possible for his purpose Gandhi may have chosen to remain anonymous knowing that his power was not increased by fame, but decreased. It is true that the experience of study in the art of conscious envisioning honestly changes what we desire. Force becomes a small concern and matters of the spirit begin to lead our intent. Envisioning flows from harmony with forgiveness, it does not flow from vengeance.[6]

I believe it is safe to say that all of us are aware of our thoughts but for most of us the awareness of the body is clouded and awareness in spirit is something we have perhaps heard about but is not something we experience daily. The process of conscious envisioning requires that we become conscious in all these areas and wipe away the cobwebs of previous experiences, habitual responses, inherited judgments, beliefs, habits, points of view, preferences, addictions and denials. This is the act of coming into our authentically true selves. Along this path of awakening is the accumulation of *coincidence* that becomes greater and greater until it becomes an accepted norm. Each time we peal away a layer, our active harmonic, the level at which we are actually envisioning becomes closer to the level of our conscious awareness. Each step of the way provides its own benefit and validation.

It may be said that at the most basic level a human being is a point of awareness within the field of physical reality. The statement 'I am' is, at the individual human level, essentially the statement 'I am aware.' When I am talking to people about mind, body and spirit and I refer to *balance,* I am talking about balanced *awareness.* The focus of awareness may be called *attention.* How much of your attention is focused upon your mind's thinking, your body's presence, or your spirit's being? Balanced awareness would be focusing an equal amount

---

[6] Reference Power vs. Force; (Chapter 3), Hawkins. Veritas 2004

of attention on the awareness of the mind, the body, and the spirit.

As manifest beings we feel we have only one point of attention. Some of us are good at splitting our attention between tasks. We cook and talk at the same time. But, if we look closely at what happens, we notice that actually we are taking our single point of attention and shifting it back and forth quickly: talking, cooking, talking, cooking, so that it appears that we are doing two things at once. However, if the roast begins to burn we find that we miss a bit of the conversation. Or if the talk becomes engrossing, the roast burns. This is the character of the attention of the mind.

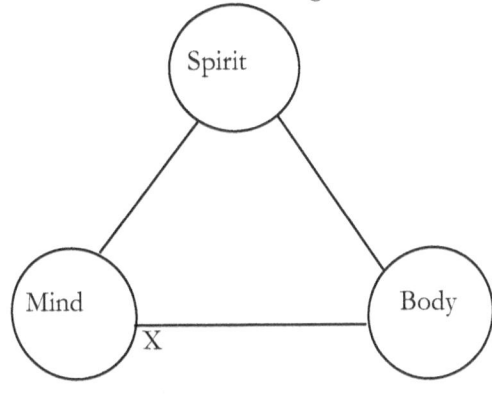

This is the way we feel when we are only consciously aware of the locus of attention as it manifests through our thoughts. Actually, we have three natural foci for our awareness, three flavors, or styles. I use the diagram below to show this.

The triangle linking the three attributes indicates that in actuality these three are all one. Most often the place of attention of individuals in the beginning of their study is at the 'X.'

Conscious awareness is nearly totally absorbed by the mind and mental processes. There is slight awareness of the body, usually represented by the awareness of discomfort or of posture. There is essentially no consciousness of spiritual awareness, thus the 'X' is outside the triangle. Remember, that I am referring only to conscious awareness. The sum total of all conscious and unconscious awareness is in balance at all times and there is ultimately no real division of awareness.

Our first task is to allow our point of attention to move somewhere away from the mind just to generate a difference of experience so that we can feel some change. The mind is often jealous of its prime position. There have been rooms full of literature written about the mind as ego and its place in our lives. There is no need. The process of envisioning will show all the strengths and weaknesses of the ego along the way. The ego is not a villain. There is no villain and no reason for vengeance.

The easiest first direction to move the point of awareness is toward the body. It has become fashionable to think of moving it toward spirit first by meditation or some other practice. This was my first instinct as well until, in my own experience, I realized that the meditative efforts that worked best for me began with training breath and, breath is a function of the body. Breath training, is the easiest and most reliable way to train your locus of awareness away from the mind toward the body. And, of course, it will produce relaxation as well by distancing the locus of attention from the mind.

Breath Training

There are many types of trained breathing, but we have two basic methods of moving air in and out of our lungs, raising our ribs and lowering our diaphragm. Rib breathing is stress breathing. It is how we evolved to come into a high state of alert. This is how we prepare for danger, get ready to run or fight. This response shuts down your immune system, stops repairing injuries, digesting food, and building bone so that your blood can go to your muscles and your brain. It is a good thing. This is how we learned to survive.

Diaphragm breathing is the opposite. This is how we are supposed to breath when there is no danger. We are supposed to spend more time in this restful breath than in stress, or rib, breathing, but in modern life we don't. In modern life our stress response is stimulated frequently and we are not good at relaxing.[7] This hyper-alert state is useful for survival, but it is firmly within the province of the ego. This creates an imbalance of awareness in mind, body and spirit, thus separating consciousness from its ability to recognize envisioning.

It is easiest to learn diaphragmatic breathing lying down on your back. The goal is conscious envisioning not complex breathing. The breath training method I use with my patients is as follows:

Basic Abdominal Breathing Technique
- With one hand on your chest and one on your abdomen
  - Take a deep breath and see which hand moves
  - Exhale fully and push any extra breath out
- Now inhale such that only your abdomen moves.
  - Inhale as deep as you can with only your abdomen moving
  - Hold this inhalation for a few moments
- Now exhale slowly and completely till your abdomen is fully pulled in.
  - Hold this for a few moments
- Repeat until you are confident that you can breathe with only your abdomen moving without your hands on your body.

When you are able to do this lying on your back roll to your side and see if you can continue with pure abdominal breathing. If so try it standing up. Next sitting, and then while doing something simple. Your goal is to be able to perform

---

[7] Herbert Benson MD The Relaxation Response HarperTorch; Reissue edition (August 1, 1976)

pure diaphragmatic breathing in whatever position or activity you find yourself. For some this is easy, for others it seems next to impossible. Everyone I have trained has gotten there eventually. The purer your abdominal breathing can be, the better; but any abdominal breathing is better than none. This is the way everyone breathes in stage four sleep. It is the way we all breathed when we were one year old. It is a matter of remembering.

It is important to take a full breath in, and hold, then to exhale more than fully, and hold. This will help to build the strength of your diaphragm and to increase the excursion of your diaphragm. Think of excursion as the full range of motion of the muscle.

Notice, in this exercise you are working your diaphragm. This is the muscle that separates your abdomen from your chest. Like any muscle it can get sore when you work it too much. This soreness will feel like a band around your chest. Don't panic; it is the same soreness you may get after a having a cough for a few days. If you really think you are having a heart attack, go get checked.

Pulse Timing

This is a method of timing your breathing cycle relative to your pulse. Since your pulse speeds up when you are burning more energy and slows down as you relax, timing breath with pulse is one way of relating the amount of air you move in a period of time to how much your body actually needs. It is also a way of making your breath cycle consistent and teaching yourself to gradually slow your breath and your metabolism.

You may take your pulse either at your wrist or at your neck. In general feel in the hollow of your wrist on the thumb side or at the hollow under the angle of your jaw. If you can't feel your pulse and if you are in the right place, you are most likely pushing too hard, rarely, not hard enough. Vary the pressure and position until you find it. If you are still having trouble ask someone who knows how to do it to find your pulse and then copy what that person did.

Now, starting with full exhalation, breathe in for a certain number of beats. If you have just sat down from walking try about four beats. If you already have been resting, try six or eight. Breathe in during those beats smoothly to a full inhalation. Then hold that position for half as many beats. Then exhale for the total you are using and hold for half. As you do, your body will begin to relax even further, and you will be able to use more beats per breath (note that you are going to use an even numbers of beats so you can divide in half).

The goal is to develop a really long breath cycle. This sends to your body a clear and commanding signal to relax deeply. This equates to moving your point of attention away from your mind toward your body. To do this more and more effectively practice moving your diaphragm very slowly and smoothly. Doing this you will develop the coordination of your diaphragm and your conscious connection to it. It is not really different from practicing any other physical movement. It takes a little time and persistence but it is not hard.

This way of training breath is very basic. Most people I have encountered have some ability to 'belly breathe' but there are some who don't really have any conscious memory of how to move that muscle. If that is you, don't worry. As I said, all of us breathe abdominally in stage four sleep. So, it is not that your body can't do it, rather that you have become unconscious of it and probably habituated to holding your stomach in. If you have insomnia it is possible that you do not reach stage four sleep often. While this may make it more foreign to breathe abdominally because you don't do so each night, by becoming able to do so consciously, especially when you are going to sleep or when you wake in the night, this ability can do wonders for your insomnia. Sometimes it is helpful to sit and practice really letting your belly relax. Occasionally, I have seen people even kneel on hands and knees and learn to let their belly hang down, but be careful in this position not to be arching your spine down.

Also, particularly with women, there is the problem of not wanting their stomach to be 'pouched' out. If this is you, remember that the point is to learn to activate your diaphragm. Once you have found it and exercised it to bring its strength back up, then you will begin breathing against a little abdominal pressure. This is more advanced and a little further than we need to go right now, but in the end this exercise of breathing against activated abdominal muscles becomes a great exercise for your stomach in every moment. Ultimately this creates a very strong beautiful abdomen and a strong resilient back.

Having started the movement away from the mind with breath training there is a second method to solidify this direction and begin the movement of attention toward spirit. It is a very basic version of Mindfulness Meditation. Again, there are many books written about mindfulness and they can be useful. But, the key at this point in the process of envisioning is to keep it basic. The desired step is to move the focus of your awareness, not to become attached to a specific method of meditation.

Mindful Meditation

A mindful meditation is entered on purpose, that is, with intent. So, you *choose* to do it. It doesn't happen by accident. It is often helpful to reinforce this by sitting in a special place or by performing some simple act. It should not be too complicated or require privacy and this trigger should be abandoned as soon as your intent is strong enough to get to the meditation without it.

The meditation begins by choosing to observe, not analyze, your thinking. This will take you from inside your thought stream to outside it. This is the act of establishing the "observer" position. If you have trouble imaging this, simply pretend that you are standing behind yourself, watching yourself. Then imagine you are standing behind your self, watching yourself think. That is it. Some of us think in words so you might imagine words going by on a screen. Some of us are more visual and so a stream of photos or short movies may feel more natural, some are more emotive, etc. In the end we all have all of these attributes of thought and a montage develops that contains elements of all types of thinking.

What will happen in the beginning is that almost immediately you will be swept back into your thought stream and you will find yourself in your usual mode of thought, problem solving, emoting, remembering, etc. This is the result of what may be called an "imperative" thought. An imperative thought is one that has sufficient allure, emotion, or interest so that you will be swept into it. At first, because you may have only a vague notion of the observer position almost all your thoughts will feel like imperatives.

When you are swept up into a thought stream you will eventually recognize that you are no longer mindfully observing. You are, remembering, emoting, or problem solving. When, not if, this happens simply and non-judgmentally use your intent to move back to the observer position. This time it will take just a little more of an imperative to sweep you back up. With a little experience in mindful meditation the intent of moving to the observer position, will solidify and it will take more and more energy for a thought to be an imperative for you.

A mindful sit lasts until three imperatives have come along. At first this won't take long. Be forgiving and loving with yourself. Judgment has absolutely no place in this experience. If you have been sitting there for ten or fifteen minutes and nothing is happening you are finished. This is not meant to be an onerous or time-consuming exercise. What is happening is that you intent to move to the observer is not strong yet and it is not moving you any perceptible distance out of your thought stream. Keep at it. The more times you set your intent the stronger it will become. I have never met anyone who persisted twice a day for a week or two who did not succeed in identifying the observer position and obtain a clear feeling of it.

I know this from personal experience. In my first attempts I didn't get anywhere. In order to strengthen my intent I chose a particular chair in my living room to sit in. When I was sitting in that chair I was doing a mindful sit. In the beginning I would get so swept up that I would be halfway out of the chair having remembered something I was supposed to do before I woke up. It was actually the physical sensation of rising from the chair that reminded me of my intent to do the sit. Sometimes, I would have to actually write down what I remembered in order to be able to let it go enough to sit again. I kept at it and now the observer position is a mainstay of my life.

Note that the observer is not a mechanism for avoiding your emotions or more difficult thoughts. The point is not to learn to *distance* but to learn to gain perspective. We will never be as good at recognizing our own battles as we are at recognizing those of others. This is not because we are at a distance from others, but because we can see them from a perspective of relative non-involvement. Often what we see in others will be a reflection of what we are attempting to avoid in ourselves. Mindfulness and the observer are not the end, but they are a beginning.[8]

---

[8] Many times in usual consciousness we are looking for the end. We feel that there is work to be done, effort to be expended, until we finally reach the end. The study of conscious envisioning is a way of life. It is not finished until life is finished. Having studied conscious envisioning for a while, it is possible that the very experience of the end of life will be quantitatively changed. No longer will fear rule that experience but it may be filled with the anticipation of

Here is what you are learning by doing mindful sits.

By identifying and strengthening the observer you are learning that you are not your thoughts. You are something different that has thoughts. Your thoughts are a tool you use, they are not your identity.

By experiencing imperatives you are learning to experience what it feels like to be swept out of your intent. What has been unconscious can now be experienced as conscious.

In returning to your intent without judgment you are learning to accept yourself and exercising compassion for yourself.

After a few weeks of doing mindful sits you will begin to recognize the feeling of being swept up in your every day life. It is exactly the same feeling as occurs during a mindful sit. Having recognized the feeling, when some stressful event occurs now, you may begin to choose whether or not to allow it to sweep you up. In this way you begin to exercise conscious choice in a realm that used to be completely unconscious.

Eventually, as you experience these techniques you will begin to be able to feel when an imperative thought is coming. This is an unusual idea: That you can become aware of the character of a thought that you haven't had yet. This awareness is a characteristic of spiritual awareness. It is connected to the notion that our thoughts are just ever so slightly in the past tense. Spiritual awareness is of and in the present moment. From the perspective of spiritual awareness you will be alert to and able to observe the process ahead of your mind. Not all imperatives are negative. Some are great fun and useful. The feeling of being swept up is part of the spice of life. Being willing and conscious of the process is even more fun. You will become aware also of deciding to end your experience of the imperative and you will able to return at will, non-judgmentally, to your original intent.

---

reunion with what we have, from the physical perspective, known only as power beyond.

Training the Breath-Observer Trigger

Once you have some ability with diaphragmatic breathing and mindful-meditation you can combine the two. That is, once you are able to take a pure diaphragmatic breath in several physical postures such as sitting, standing and while doing something, such as reading. And, when you are able to reach the observer position and know confidently that you are there. At that point you may begin to combine the intent to move to the observer with taking a diaphragmatic breath. This way, your breath training becomes an anchor to hold you in the observer position, and the simple act of a pure diaphragmatic breath will trigger the movement of your awareness to the observer position.

In combining breath and the intent to observe you are learning to switch to the observer at will in times of difficulty and stress.

Once you have set your Breath-Observer Trigger it is important that you continue to train it. The trigger is a simple Pavlovian Trigger.[9] If you use it only in stressful times, but don't continue to reinforce the trigger in restful times, the trigger will eventually become unreliable. Like any trained attribute we need to continue to practice if we want to continue to be skilled.

Now you have a fully assembled tool that can change your response to stress. You may choose to allow an imperative

---

[9] Pavlov was the psychologist that trained animals to associate a stimulus with getting food, or eventually any pleasurable experience. He found that even a painful stimulus would be endured if it had a conditioned pleasure experience associated with it. However, he also found that not continuing the conditioning would cause the strength of the trigger to eventually degrade and then disappear.

to activate for you, or you may choose to put it on hold, or dismiss it altogether. When we have the perspective of choice, many seemingly imperative elements of our lives turn out not to be so imperative. Prior to being fully immersed in the imperative we have options and there is no feeling of desperation. It is one thing to need to take a breath after you have submerged in the water. It is more empowered to choose whether or not you want to jump in.

Review Concepts for Envisioning Tier Two

With breath training we move our locus of attention away from the mind toward the body. This attention to the body is not a subtraction from the mind but rather an awakening of the attention of the body. Then, with mindfulness and placing attention on the 'observer,' we will be pulling the locus in the only direction it 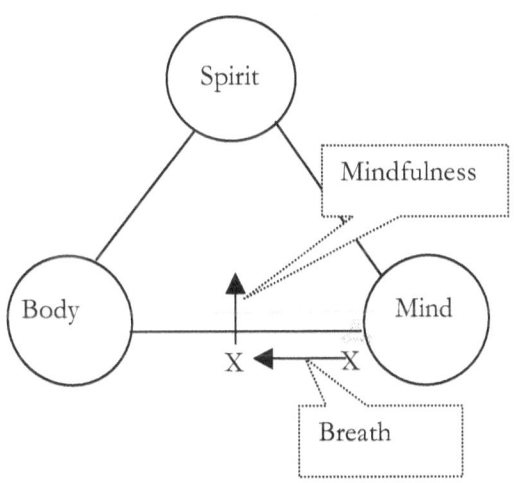 can go, toward spirit. In this way we are moving the point of our attention toward the balance point of mind, body and spirit. There is a feeling to being at this point. It is comfortable in a way that makes sense deeply inside. Being at the balance point of mind, body and spirit provides a comfort that overcomes physical or mental discomfort. And, it opens the connection to power beyond that makes envisioning possible.

It is an important aspect of the process of Envisioning that in deciding to breathe abdominally there is a thought (to do it) and a decision (to do it) all processed by the mind. In mindfulness the original intent is formed in conscious thought, in the mind. Both times the mind is involved. The mind is a very useful tool. We have, in modern times, come to be very good with our minds. So good, in fact, that we have confused it with our actual identity. We are not our thoughts. We are not a summation of our thoughts. We are a triune: "mind-body-spirit." The mind is not supreme. Even from the most basic experience of conscious breathing and finding the observer, we can say that we are much more than just our thoughts.

A study of these basic steps will form a basis for the first level of consciousness in envisioning. This is the first "conscious Harmonic." In tier one having simply read the concepts you had done all you needed to do. In this, the second tier, having read the words you only know *what* you will need to do. We are at the first point in this book about the art of conscious envisioning where you actually have to *do* something. From here, if you are not experiencing what I am writing about, you will only know what I am *saying*. You will not be able to understand what I *mean*. I chose to call envisioning an 'art of conscious' not just because it is beautiful but because it is essentially an *experience*. It is the pure embodiment of experience. Envisioning is experience and nothing else. It can be talked about, and written about, but nothing of its essence is contained in the words used or the thoughts exchanged. The use of reading is similar to the use of a map. It can help you know how to get there, but it can neither move you nor convey what it is to be there.

First Envisioning, The Flow

At this point you have an incomplete, mostly mental understanding of envisioning. The way to build on this is to begin seeking experience. Envisioning will begin as a task and become a natural part of your life. If we could remember our first breath coming out of the womb we would remember it as a task. Prior to that first breath all our needs had been met without the slightest effort from ourselves. Perhaps in the womb we didn't even recognize ourselves as separate or as needing anything, even air, but we found ourselves pushed out into the world. Whether we were stimulated by a slap or a cuddle, we found that there was a need that grew each second. It forced us to take that first breath. It was a bit of a struggle to expand lungs that had never been expanded with air before. For a little while it was a task, but soon it became natural.

This is the way it will be with envisioning. To envision consciously will be new. Up until this moment you have been cradled, for better or worse, in the unconscious envisioning of the collective. Now, it has come time for the first breath of conscious envisioning.

I have said that it is unlikely that you just stumbled into reading this. You are seeking conscious envisioning for a specific reason. I accept that each of us has an agenda. You and I are the same in this. Our agendas are not a coincidence. Just as with mine, your agenda is the driving force for your desire to come into your ability to envision consciously. However, though this agenda is dear to your soul, it should not become the conscious focus of your first envisioning. How sad, right? Your ego may jump right up and complain. I know mine did. "What good is it then?," my ego said. Often our driving agenda has something to do with our personal health. It is dear to us and is loaded with emotion. I have witnessed many times that health comes as a result when a Consciously Envisioned future requires it. As your ability grows to consciously envision and as you build faith through experience you will find your personal reasons for living. At that point your agenda for personal health will most likely take care of itself.

For your first envisioning I would prefer that you take something much less difficult, much less specific, but in its own way even more powerful. I will suggest something but you may find that you need to take your own road. There are no rules in envisioning and there is no authority over you.[10]

I will suggest that you envision what I call "The Flow." Right away your mind is going to tell you that it doesn't know what the heck *The flow* is! And, I'm going to say to your mind, *correct*! Because, I only want your mind to have a vague idea of what is going on. It is already too full of itself and too jealous of its control of your identity. I wouldn't be surprised if, right now, as you are reading this, you have a vague sense of desire to put the book down. Underestimating the mind and its desire to remain in supreme control is one of the first struggles we all have in approaching conscious envisioning. So, tell your mind that its job from now on is to *direct* the show, not to *be* the show. If you give your mind a specific job it will be happy. That is what it is built for.

The Flow is a state of being where you are in a cooperative relationship with all that surrounds you. Surrounding includes the thoughts surrounding you (mind), the space, objects, and people surrounding you (body), and the energy surrounding you (spirit). Your relationship with all of this I refer to as the flow. In the relationship we seek within the flow the things you need appear to you. The people you need come to you. The circumstances of your day seem to work out. It feels as if you are being given a gift and there is no thought of worthiness or deservingness. There is no obligation. It is simply as if the wind is blowing in your direction. The resulting feeling is gratitude.

So, as I suggest using the flow as the focus of our first envisioning together, I will also suggest that your mind understands all it needs to at this point. It may still niggle for more details, more explanation, but simply let your head know that from now on its job is to read the words, interpret them, and that is it!

---

[10] Note that power beyond self is not an "authority." A discussion of the absence of hierarchy is further on in the text.

Thus, the mind makes the decision to envision consciously. Next, it brings an 'understanding' to the task and then it must admit that there is more than it can understand, that must be experienced. At this point the mind takes on an observing role.

The next place the attention goes is to the body, through breathing. Take a deep breath. Let it out slowly. Place your attention on the feeling of your body breathing. Use your breathing as the window into your body and how it exists in this moment. From time to time the ideas of the mind may come to you. As in our practice with mindful meditation passively and non-judgmentally, direct the mind to the notion of the flow and ask, what it would feel like, in your body, to be in the flow. Allow, the expression of this feeling to seep into your body without your mind to attempting to describe it. The idea is to simply observe. Like the feeling of warmth your body understands it; your mind does not need to analyze. At this point you are imagining it. You are wondering what it feels like. Your body is answering. The flow is actually something that your body is familiar with, something it remembers, like it remembers how to breathe. There is no struggle. Just breathe and allow the idea of the flow to reside in you.

When you have trained yourself even slightly in connecting mindfulness with breath, you will naturally begin to drift into the position of the observer. This will happen slowly and without effort. This place from which you are observing is in the direction of spirit from the mind-body interface. As you are observing yourself in mind and body allow yourself to accept that the vantage point from which you are observing is closer to spirit than is your normal state of being. It is like backing up into spiritual perspective. Bring part of your attention to the notion that in the universe you are unique and very special, but you are not the absolute power. Bring that part of your attention to your undefined notion of a power beyond yourself. Allow into your imagining an awareness of that power flowing through you like a current and flowing into what you are observing.

The feeling for me is like the feeling of being in a room. In the room is my usual self, my mind and my body, as I commonly know them. My vantage of observation is by the door to the room or by a window and I open it to let power beyond the room enter. Sometimes I imagine the feeling as a light flooding in, sometimes as a wind. The more I have done this, the more it is simply the feeling of a shift, or a change. The change is not here or there, it is everywhere, and it is accompanied by a feeling of gratitude. When I feel this I move toward that feeling. This is the feeling of the completion of the envisioning.

Notice that as the process of envisioning unfolds, the object of the envisioning disappears. If you hold onto the object, or plan, for the results of the envisioning, you will wind up trying. This is an unavoidable consequence of holding the object tightly. I would never even attempt to *convince* my mind of the fact of an envisioning. Envisioning is always about more than was originally intended. The object always winds up being just the beginning, the impetus. This is some of the magic. I don't analyze the results of my envisioning. The mind cannot understand envisioning. Analysis seems to set up an unconsciously counter-envisioned intent or current of its own. To analyze, I must also expect the opposite. Instead, I end by observing gratitude purely, without expectation, forgetting even that I consciously envisioned at all.

In the beginning of your practice, the process described as envisioning will take a few minutes. There are times when I revel in the process and give it lots of time, which, for me, is about twenty minutes. Most often now it is a few seconds. Envisioning is simple. It operates deeper than words or descriptions, so don't let my words stand in your way. Use what I have written to find your own way. Observe your results and fine tune your methods. Learn to quiet your mind and listen to your body. Accept your doubts and allow all your humanity to show. Before long you will come to your own individual path.

I started out by saying that no one needed to learn how to envision. Everyone is doing it unconsciously in every moment. In my own way of understanding, this is what moments are made of. You now know the concepts, the notions of a mind-body-spirit harmonic, and you have walked through an envisioning. The tools are simple but we know that putting them into practice is not so easy.

Remember the story of my night with the bow-drill? I have now taught many people to make fire with this primitive apparatus. The magic of the bow drill is that it is so closely linked to the Spirit of the Earth. A student's first fire often comes somewhat easily. For me, observing as the teacher, it is clear that this first fire is a gift from the Earth. So many times I have watched a person easily succeed once only to be unable to make a second fire for a long time. It is with this second fire that the student must take his or her own conscious steps into the spiritual relationship with the Earth through the bow-drill. I tell them that the Earth requires each of us to be at our best in this relationship. It is not simply a physical skill. To this day, to reliably make fire with a bow-drill, I must do my very best in exactly that moment in time.

Envisioning itself is a natural and effortless process. We do not have to work to do it. But, to become conscious of what we are doing we do have to uncover the myriad of reasons and methods we use to block ourselves from our own awareness. We benefit not only as individuals, but also as a collective, each time an unconscious block falls away allowing our increased awareness. As human beings we often have the best of intentions in mind for others and ourselves, but often, we are unable to manifest the results of our good intentions. This is the struggle and the joy of our physical journey. The work is not in the actual envisioning; rather it is in getting out of the way of ourselves. This is where the work is and also the fun. It is through the enjoyment of knowing ourselves fully and honestly that we can come to experience fully. The results of this experience will lead us on. This is what I mean by, "in the end, only the results count."

The Art Of Conscious Envisioning

Chapter 2

Whatever It Takes

Having lived within the art of envisioning for the past ten years I am familiar with what happens next. Just as with the bow drill fire there may be some spontaneous, early successes to lead us on our first efforts at envisioning may work better than we expect. This is especially true if the objects of our first envisionings are kept nonspecific like the flow, but there is a desire to do more, to become more specific and just wishing for it doesn't make it happen. Early successes are followed rather abruptly by either disappointment or disillusionment. The Earth is willing to allow fire to an immature bow drill student once or twice. Power beyond is initially willing to reach through our confusion to find the intention we are sending and help our envisioning along, once or twice. These experiences are the experiences of interacting consciousness. They are the breadcrumb trail leading toward the expansion and the joining of consciousness. For those who see the trail and do not return to the illusion of meaningless coincidence there comes a strong commitment and a desire to go deeper. From here on we will need this commitment.

When I began my study of animal tracking I was in a class of more than one hundred students. On the last day of the class Tom Brown was about to start talking to us about tracking mice across the gravel driveway. While he was waiting for the group to assemble he was crouching down looking at the sparse grass growing in the middle of the two-track driveway. As he looked up his face was lit with an excited energy that caught my attention. It was as if he was assessing the group to see if anyone there could share what he had seen. He pulled out a popsicle stick and excitedly began writing on it. I knew he had found a track and was writing on the stick what the track was. When he finished he pushed the popsicle stick in the ground marking the track and stood up. He went on about his lecture not mentioning it again.

When later we were turned loose to try the exercise with the mice and the gravel I took a moment to look at the track he had marked. It said; right front foot, yearling female deer, 3:15 am, this morning. On that day I could barely even see that there was a track there let alone pull any information from it, but I imagined what it would be like to see it as Tom Brown did with all that information exposed. I realized that his excitement had not been about being able to see the track as mine would have been. Such awareness had long become routine to him. He was excited that the deer would come into that place which was between a barn filled with over a hundred of his students and the farm house filled with his helpers and teachers. In that, I believe, he felt some acceptance of his school and his teaching by the deer. It was not a coincidence that the deer was there or that the track presented itself to his awareness.

That moment galvanized in me a desire to expand my awareness to the point where I could see the signs of nature as he did. I knew this would require a commitment of time and energy, but I was ready to do whatever it took to open my eyes to what had become natural to him.

About three years later, I was walking a path through the field by my house. On this particular section of the path, which was grown high with field plants on both sides, the sun chanced to angle all the way to the ground. While I was walking I looked down and noticed a line of fox tracks along the trail. Even before I knelt down to be sure I knew that the tracks were from that early morning and that they were of a red fox probably female. The awareness had come to me naturally and surely. At that point I remembered the look on Tom Brown's face that day in the driveway. There was no way back on that day in class that I could have shared his awareness but years later I was coming closer.

This is the way it is with the study of envisioning. We can become aware it is possible and then we will have to choose how far we will have the commitment to go ourselves. There will always be the option to stop learning. We will always have the option of even returning to the belief that it is impossible to know that the deer really was there at exactly three fifteen am. Or, we can continue to learn perhaps one day to find that point of knowing ourselves.

In chapter one we studied the entrance to the triangle of mind body and spirit. By breath training we brought our attention toward balance between the mind and the body. Then, with mindfulness and seeking the observer, we moved into the triangle toward balancing mind body and spirit. Now we will look at the climb toward that balance in detail. It will require some setting aside of old ideas and the acceptance of new ones. In fact, I don't really think of it as moving into a triangle. I think of climbing a pyramid. A pyramid is a structure that sits on a firm base and, as it rises, it remains in balance becoming ever more refined. At the very top of the pyramid is the cap-stone. This is the pinnacle, where the sides are united and the structure is brought to balance in a single point. As long as the capstone remains the pyramid will shed the elements letting nothing disturb its strength, but the capstone cannot be placed early. The whole of the pyramid must be ready for this final step of completion.

As it becomes clear that Envisioning requires more of us than a superficial effort, we are confronted with a test of our willingness. It is not a simple task. While there is a path, there is no instruction book whose details are common to us all. We must be willing to do *whatever it takes* to bring our art of conscious envisioning to the next level. This is where the path of awakening becomes the most difficult. Perhaps it is unfortunate that the most difficult part of the trail is right near the beginning. Or, perhaps it is good because you will not be lured in by the promise of a 'quick fix.' Regardless of how far you travel on the path toward conscious envisioning you will benefit. But, it is important to remember that after this first hard step, the second is easier and the third easier still. It is the initial change of belief that comes the hardest. That is the letting go and the surrender.

When Is An Illness An Illness?

It is necessary to admit that we are not just uncomfortable with the status quo of who we are and how we are proceeding in life, we are dying of it. We must let go of the idea that because most people are at a similar state, it is the natural state of human-ness. We must consider that there is more available to us and become willing to change. We have become comfortable and accustomed to a form of thinking and being that is unhealthy and that is blocking us from the awakening we are looking for. For me, I was unable to accomplish any letting go or surrender, until I came to accept that the normal patterns of awareness to which I was accustomed, were not only unhealthy, they represented a disease.

This is a radical thought; that normal human consciousness is diseased. In general, health is defined as that which is most common. Why would we consider applying a diagnosis of disease to the majority condition? There are several reasons. Admittedly as a physician I may be more comfortable with the concept of disease than lay people, but consider the following points.

First, we are all naturally resistant to accepting that we have an actual illness but when a diagnosis is given and a treatment is prescribed we are more likely to accept the treatment if we believe we actually have a problem than if we think of it as a recommendation for health maintenance. In essence the diagnosis provides urgency.

Second, when we focus on and accept the notion that we have a disease we can then focus on what it might be to become healthy. Human beings are very adaptable. We very rapidly become accustomed to a diseased state and can come to consider it normal. Imagine what it would be like to believe that to die is not normal. Imagine that to be conscious of everlasting life and to be consciously aware that the physical phase of life comes and goes at your will is actually the most natural and healthy state of human consciousness. Sound ridiculous? Sure it does if considered from our more usual state of having accepted death as indecipherable, inevitable and normal.

Third, when a diagnosis is applied it can help us to define a treatment model. There is a disease that we are very familiar with that has all the attributes of our blocks to conscious envisioning. It remains a very difficult disease to treat but not because we do not know how to proceed. The difficulty is not that the treatment is unknown or ineffective, but rather that it is completely up to the person who is suffering. Just as with envisioning, no one can require that you awaken. The road to awakening requires exactly what our model disease requires, that the seeker voluntarily act with a level of willingness unheard of within normal human affairs.

A diagnosis is essentially a statement that a given situation is sufficiently similar to a previously observed group of experiences that predictions can be made. By this we can say that a person has pneumonia if we observe a cough, a fever, shortness of breath, and crackles when we listen to his lungs. Further we can predict that without treatment with an antibiotic he is likely to be ill for a long time and quite possibly die.[11] The cough, fever, shortness of breath and crackles are the group of experiences. They are quite unaffected by whether we call them pneumonia or not, but naming the group of experiences helps us to recognize it and once we have categorized the experience in this way it helps us to know what to do. This is basically how medicine is practiced. It is about comparing one group of experiences to another. But, human beings are all individuals, none are the same and even each experience of pneumonia is unique. The group of experiences has to be generalized to fit more than one individual.

It has long been my belief that, in the practice of medicine with our individual patients, we doctors would be better off to avoid giving a diagnosis and just concern ourselves with what is the next thing we should do. In this case of cough, fever, shortness of breath and crackly lungs, giving antibiotics should be considered. Whether I call the process pneumonia won't affect whether the individual gets well and in fact if the situation changes, the fact that I have named it pneumonia, will make it harder for me to detect the changes. There is a tendency to categorize and then stop observing.

---

[11] There are viral pneumonias of course that do not require an antibiotic.

That said, I find myself considering the benefit of comparing our experience of awakening to conscious envisioning to the experience of known disease experiences. As in the situation of comparing the blocks to awakening to conscious envisioning to another situation where a block in awareness is the basis of the pathology. It is possible that the treatment for the older, more familiar, situation may apply to the new one. It is also possible that the root cause of the old situation is related to the root cause of the new one.

Our challenge in awakening to conscious envisioning is that we must become willing to accept, without judgment that, that what we have always taken to be normal, is in fact, not normal at all. This characteristic is exactly the same for our old known disease and for our blocks to conscious envisioning. And, in both cases, it is not a character defect or a sign of inadequacy; it is a disease that has developed over a very long period of time in nearly the whole of humanity. We must see that although this way of being is very common, it is actually an unnatural state. Accepting that what is usually considered normal consciousness and its resulting effects are actually the symptoms of a disease helps us to think about what this disease might be. In the case of pneumonia, the disease is a function of an infections organism being present in the lungs where it should not be. In the case of the disease that blocks conscious envisioning, it is a function of attention. Our attention is the directing, or focusing function, of our awareness. In the disease of our attention, our focus has become completely attached to the things of the physical world. In all but the most rare of circumstances we are paying rapt attention to the level of awareness that perceives the physical world around us and no attention to anything else. This has become such a common mode of attention-focus that it seems as if it is the only level upon which our attention operates. Our acceptance that this as an unnatural state that it is a state of disease, is required for us to awaken.

Just as it is natural for us to become diseased with a cold, this condition of diseased attention is usual. I am not saying that each of us doesn't need to go through a phase where things physical consume our attention, but conscious envisioning is about awakening from that phase into the next. When an individual stops maturing at any childhood stage there is usually a disease that is causing their arrested growth. In our modern day times we do not think of these individuals as inferior, rather we acknowledge that some process beyond their control is preventing them from becoming adult. In the past these individuals were stigmatized. Today that stigma has lessened and the amount of judgment applied is reduced. This has helped us to accept these individuals into society and we even find that they do contribute though not in the same ways as those who have developed normally.

In awakening to conscious envisioning we are interested not only in changing the details of our experience we are seeking to change our entire relationship with life. In a sense we are seeking to grow up into a new phase of our relationship with life, especially physical life. It is not a usual way of thinking. We are not talking about changing the events or the qualities directly. We are talking about changing the source and the reason for everything. That our normal way of focusing attention is a disease and not the only way may be hard to accept. The only way we can know that this is true is to become willing to accept it, or at least to suspend your disbelief long enough, to grow to the point where another way of focusing attention becomes known. It is a test of willingness that opens the door. The question is; how badly do you want it and what are you willing to invest? Are you willing to give up your whole idea of yourself in order to seek a new self and a new relationship with life? If not, life can, and will, go on just as it has. There are many other options to believe in. No one says you have to use this one or any one at all. In fact, life is arranged to allow you to remain in childhood-awareness as long as you choose. There may be consequences for human beings as a whole if none of us awaken, but any given individual may continue on unchanging as long as desired.[12]

---

[12] In the terms of reincarnation this may include many lifetimes.

There are hundreds, if not more, books and seminars on creating your own future, living life from spiritual source, the notion of the now, and more. Some of these stem from ancient traditions, others are relatively new renditions. Many, or even all of them, may hold elements of truth. But, I have yet to see a revolution in the way we live our lives. The spiritual realm has not balanced with the physical realm. Except for technological progress the bulk of humanity still basically goes about its life in the same way it always has. There has been societal progress away from persecution and that allows each of us to consider new ideas more freely. Violence in general is given less tolerance in the world as a whole though there are clear exceptions. I do believe that we generally care for our children better and that each generation improves. There are places in the world that are ahead in some ways and other places that are ahead in other ways, but the basic process of living within a physical system that we manipulate with our hands and minds remains unchanged.[13]

Sometimes reality does seem to sway toward spirit for a small number of individuals. You may hear this at any number of parties or polite discussions. The effects of energy work through massage may change an individual's experience, for a short while. Sometimes, a life threatening experience will awaken a special seeming awareness for a while. Many who have attended spiritual retreats or seminars feel changed, but most return quickly to their status. What is happening? Is this just the effect of a temporary delusion as the scientific community, and doctors, would have it? Or is something else going on? Is it that we can experience our disease of attention fixation differently in a supportive environment but to actually overcome it, is more difficult? Is it that envisioning at any level of consciousness has an effect, but only envisioning at the deepest levels actually creates real and lasting change?

---

[13] That it has not always been so is a debate of prehistory. Spaulding, <u>Life And Teachings Of The Masters of the Far East </u>De Vorss, 1964

If you come into a room that has blue paint on the walls and you paint it red have you changed the fact that the walls are still also blue? If you look superficially at the wall it will appear red and with good paint it may last a while but underneath the walls are blue. The fact that you think of the walls as red is a result of your focus of attention on the surface and your denial that underneath they are blue. It is also possible that under the blue layer the walls are also yellow. It is a good bet that under the yellow is white and then paper and then plaster and wood in our modern housing. What is real? Are the walls red, blue, yellow, white, or plaster and wood? Clearly, in the case of walls they are all these. Why don't we choose to perceive them as they actually are?

In the case of our personal reality, in the face of an increasing awareness of coincidence, the condition is that the adherence of the outer layers is less solid than a good coat of paint. Pretending that surface awareness is good enough is popular, but this pretense isn't sustainable after attention to coincidence begins. The painted over experiences of judgments and beliefs begin to crack off and reveal the deeper substrate. If we keep painting fast enough and often enough with thick enough paint we may be able keep up the appearance that things are under control for a while. The focus of attention to the superficial was fun while it lasted, but now it is becoming work. Even though maintaining superficial attention is normal, common and accepted, what is the cost and what is the purpose? The purpose is the maintenance of a state of being that is ultimately diseased and the cost is that it is doomed to end in confusion and fear. This set of experiences is the same with our model disease and with our experience of awakening to conscious envisioning.

Once I asked a hundred patients this question. "Do you want to live forever"? Only one person answered yes. He was a crusty gentleman farmer who came in at age eighty-two after cutting himself in his garden. His eyes sparkled when he answered my question. I could see that he had outgrown thinking about the future and was one of the rare individuals who lived truly in the now and knew its connection to forever.

There was no fear in his answer. I knew I had met someone to whom not only did I have nothing to teach, but with whom I was now the student. His approach to life was simple and as I sewed his hand I drank it in. He talked about what he loved and what he wanted to get back to. The feeling I got was that he was always moving toward what he wanted. To him forever was right now.

As for the other ninety-nine people who answered no, when I asked my follow up question: "How long do you want to live?" None of them said, ten more years, or till I'm ninety. There were no quantitative values to their answers. Instead they said, till I see my grandchildren or, I'd like to live long enough to ... some activity. "A while longer" was the most common response seconded by, "Well, I'm not ready to go yet!" The feeling I got from all these patients was that they were running from death hoping to stay ahead till some abstract goal was reached. Usually, I saw that this goal was more like the carrot hanging in front of the donkey's nose to keep them moving rather than anything that would actually provide completion and wholeness to their lives. In other words when dealing with the concept of our own deaths, we, as a group, have some difficulty with specifics.

It has taught me a great deal to be involved with many elderly individuals as they come closer and closer to their last day. I'd like to say that I have witnessed the tranquil preparation for the ultimate spiritual transition, but I cannot. What I have seen is that the vast majority become more and more fearful. In the end, most of the time, the fear of death that has been hidden by the distraction of the physical carrot is now clear and present. Many individuals are no longer heading toward anything, now they are totally consumed with running from pain and death. On the occasions when I felt it was safe to ask them about this they would usually deny it. "I'm ready", they'll say, but their choices and actions speak differently. Instead of opening into death, family resources, medical resources, any and all resources, are consumed at whatever rate necessary to maintain even a painful life as long as possible.

My viewpoint from the emergency department undoubtedly skews my observation away from those who have chosen a more tranquil transition and therefore do not present repeatedly in extremis. It is also true that the process of modern medicine, in general, does not support spiritual growth or spiritual transition, but I do believe personally, that this is an accurate reflection of the collective unconscious' envisioning into reality. This is to say that even though we recognize that at some point we are going to have to deal with the issue, we still put it off with increasing amounts of effort. This is another experience that is shared between our model disease and our effort to awaken.

It is completely true that this is the collective norm in our present society but this is an artifact of our times. The current generation of elderly is the first group who has had to face the problem of an artificially supported life that extends significantly beyond the time of physical capability. In the not really very distant past to lie in bed for any period of time was to die naturally. Now, a full complement of medications exists to deal with all the problems associated with being incapacitated and delay the finality of death indefinitely. These are not even thought of as extraordinary measures anymore. They are standard treatments such as anti-coagulation for blood clots, diuretics for fluid retention and heart failure, a host of blocking agents that lower the work that the body has to do. Ultimately the failing body is placed in a sort of artificial partial hibernation so that the events that once naturally occurred to end life no longer occur. The result is hundreds of thousands of individuals living in a physical state that didn't previously exist. The nursing home industry is testimony to this. In the past the elderly died at home and while it may have taken months, it did not take years or decades as it often does now. There is no fault to be discovered and no one is to blame for this. It is a new experience, but it is important to recognize that for most of human history this situation has not been possible. The importance is that this is one of the vague but clearly present motivating factors for the millions of people who are now attempting to find another path. And it is one of the defining characteristics of the set of experiences we are coming to diagnose.

In the past the elderly were seen as a precious resource of wisdom and experience. They still are, of course. In the past, part of that wisdom was an acknowledgement of what the tribe as a whole required to survive. We lived in small groups where, if too many resources were given to those who no longer hunted or gathered food, no one would survive. This wisdom was held in the whole but also each elder made their own choice. For a youth to enforce such a choice upon their elder was unthinkable but for an elder not to be aware of and responsible for this choice was equally impossible. Currently, the connection between resources and consequences has become obscured by the size of our tribe and by the richness of our times but the ultimate truth of the situation remains the same.

In less recent but still modern times the big jumps in longevity have come from public health actions such as plentiful food sources and sewers. Medical science provided its first contributions with vaccinations and antibiotics. These were relatively inexpensive innovations. Only recently, in the past twenty years, has the effect of the current regimen of ten medications, heart catheterizations, chemotherapy, pacemakers and transplants been felt. The current generation of elderly is the first to experience the effect of high-tech, mega expense, medical care. The explosion of nursing home residents wasn't planned nor the cost anticipated. It was a hidden effect that the science of their generation, and mine, has produced. This is not comfortable for them to consider nor for the generations that will need to pay. Even though the problems are inevitable, even though we know that this future is not sustainable, we cannot quite bring ourselves to deal with it openly. This is another direct parallel between our situation and our model disease.

Those of us who are fifty are watching this. We know that we are heading down the same path. The booming advent of the long-term health insurance industry is a signpost if any is needed. The medical industry is very pleased with itself. Every third advertisement on television is for health care of some sort. The amount of the gross national product consumed by health care is still increasing without any boundary. We see in our elderly what the results are but we think, somehow, it will be different for us. Most people haven't woken up to the fact that what is advertised and sold as health care isn't even *health* care. It is *illness* care. This fact is a main element in the diagnostic picture we are building. Instead of cough, fever, shortness of breath equaling pneumonia, the picture is the inability to look clearly and specifically at the difficult issues in our lives and lifestyles, our ability to hide the truth from ourselves by simply denying that it exists and the drastically increasing costs, on all levels, of sustaining that denial.

Certainly, it isn't that *no one* has noticed. In fact, I would bet that if you are still reading this you have woken up to these facts. However, the voices do remain few. This is not a surprise. It is a symptom of the problem. This is the same disease of awareness that keeps envisioning at the individual level from becoming conscious as it plays out on the communal or societal level.

Even if you choose to stop your journey toward consciousness in envisioning at this point, the elements explored in chapter one will continue to create more comfort, harmony and health for you. There is no mandate to go further. You may choose another direction such as to study conscious dreaming, attend an inspirational talk, spend a week at a silent retreat or read another book. There is no good or bad, no success or failure. It is all simply experience and it is valid in its own right. Some experiences we are ready to seek and some experiences we are not. Accepting the parallel diagnosis as I am suggesting is not mandatory in any way. As I have said, the first step toward conscious envisioning is clearly the hardest.

I have tried through many years to make this phase of the journey more palatable by avoiding the subject of diseased attention. The results are always poor or disastrous. I can only tell you what I know. I have to be honest because that is what the experience of envisioning demands. I admit that this phase is a challenge and it is not for everyone. I am emphasizing that challenge by writing that we must accept that we are suffering from a disease. To move on toward awakening to consciousness in envisioning, in the only way I know, we must become capable of accepting this challenge completely and we must do so without the slightest taint of judgment.

The prize of conscious envisioning is grand and sublime but the challenge is correspondingly humbling. To become conscious and purposeful in envisioning we must accept that we have been envisioning all along. Attention is the primary tool of envisioning. Placing attention in service of obtaining awareness of the physical world to the exclusion of every other possibility is where we begin. It is not that we must learn to expand our awareness, but to stop restricting it. Thus, we must accept that we have been envisioning not just from an unconscious state, but from a state of conscious denial.

This is the disease. It is placing our attention in service of the physical world, denying that there is anywhere else or anything else to be aware of. In this way we deny our awareness of the whole process of envisioning. We are then free to conclude that the events of the world occur in isolation from us as separate occurrences over which we have no control.

To think of this situation as a disease of attention affecting our personal awareness of envisioning rather than as ordinary consciousness or a habit is our challenge. This means that everything that is happening to you and everything that has happened must be accepted as part of your own envisioning. We do not want to accept that we are involved with everything that has happened or is happening from the grand to the minute so we deny it all and then forget that our denial. To accept this awareness is to accept our role in everything, even the events that tear at our hearts, but until we do the process of history will simply grind on unchanged. Just as the individual life of limited awareness does finally come to its end so too may the collective.

Understand that your doing and your envisioning are not the same things. To accept our personal role is not to become responsible for all that happens. In physically doing an act you participate from the level of your ego alone. You have the choice to do something or not to do something and for these actions or inactions you are responsible. In envisioning you act and have always acted in partnership with power beyond. You don't have the choice to envision or not. Your, our, only choice is to become conscious and then to envision consciously. Though we absolutely don't understand all the reasons for all the events we have formed in our lives, though the how or the why are often beyond our current understanding, to become conscious of envisioning we must accept that every event has its meaning and none of it, is or was *ever* an accident. All of it exists within each of us and all of it was done in conscious or unconscious partnership with power beyond.

This giving up the notion of 'unimportant coincidence' or that "shit just happens" is hard, but in order to change we must. There is no way of being in halfway. This is another parallel. In ancient legends, when the gods walked the Earth and challenged each other through human affairs, the tragic and seemingly purposeless events that happened were explained as conflicts between the gods. Human beings were just part of the playing field. By imagining a host of powers beyond, the ancients solved the problem of understanding the terror they witnessed in their lives. Today, the notion of multiple deities who are in competition with each other is not widely held. Most people, when they think of power beyond, have some notion of a single source. Thus to accept that 'shit just happens' is either to put limits on the power of this source such that some things happen that are outside of its control or it is to believe in vengeance. These beliefs are another parallel with our model disease. Recovery cannot begin until it is accepted that there is no nepharious other who is causing all our problems. There is *no* truth to vengeance in our model disease or in our journey toward conscious envisioning.

The challenge of accepting nonjudgmental responsibility is also to accept *response – ability*, the ability to respond, to what comes next. This does not demand a specific response from any given individual. As I said in the beginning, there is no rulebook. There is no authority of appeal higher than yourself. Your current version of power beyond is simply that, your current version. Only your results along the path can inform your choice. This challenge to awaken demands simply whatever it takes for *you*, for each of us. The process of awakening may have similarities but the details will be different for each of us. This is the final parallel. Even though there is a path and similarities to our journeys and even though journeying in community and hearing about each other's experiences is helpful, ultimately, we must each find our own path inside ourselves.

Accepting Our Diagnosis

Many of us are imbedded in experiences that we would never choose from our logical frame of awareness. To accept that we are choosing and creating exactly these circumstances at some level, to accept this responsibility and to begin to seek out awareness on that level is exciting, terrifying and humbling in the extreme. Conscious envisioning is profoundly simple but it is not easy. The difficulty is not due to something external or to some structure that is beyond our control. The difficulty is *most difficult* precisely because it is completely within our control. To become aware of this is to see the challenge clearly. Once the challenge is accepted it may not be possible to retreat again to our previous comfortable blindness. Once the fruit is tasted it is not forgotten. We know this truth deep within our unconscious and so acceptance is felt to be dangerous, improbable, and difficult. It is not the fall from Eden that was challenging, it is the return. It is not the diseased state that is difficult to maintain it is the discovery of recovery. The fact that this feeling of difficulty is ultimately an illusion cannot be known until the challenge is accepted and navigated.

I stated that the function of a diagnosis was in its utility for motivating us and suggesting a course of treatment. The disease pattern I have been referring to models our resistance to awakening is well known and parallels our situation exactly. This disease is common, perhaps one of the most common diseases known to man. It is present in every modern society though that has not always been so. It is also a disease of attention and its treatment prescribes a radical change in the mode and method of paying attention. As such the treatment is solely under the control of the person afflicted. The treatment course can be seen as demanding, but primarily this is in its first steps where acceptance and surrender to the process of treatment is required. If taken rigorously the treatment supports a good prognosis for recovery and the afflicted can come to a new state of being very superior to the former state. In diseases of attention relapse can always occur, old choices can always be revisited, but never again with uncontested results. Once steps toward healing are taken the disease never again feels the same. Our model pattern is a disease that carries with it still, a societal stigma that is necessary to overcome and so it fulfills our need for commitment and for overcoming judgment. Our model disease is the disease of we name addiction. Addiction is a disease supported by unconscious denial every bit as complete as our denial of envisioning. Addiction is a disease where the attention of the afflicted becomes totally focused on the object of obsession, to the exclusion of all else, similar to our obsession with the physical plane. Addiction is also a disease of ego consciousness that is overcome by surrendering to a power beyond.

Classically, the diagnosis of addiction is applied to physical behaviors such as gambling or the consumption of a substance such as alcohol. To extend this diagnosis to our situation is to say that the focus of attention on the physical plane to the exclusion of all else represents an addiction of attention to the physical world. Placing our attention in service of the physical world and denying all else is, in practice, exactly parallel to an addict's act of placing all attention on the next fix or the next role of the dice.

Classical addiction is a disease of focal insanity. In all other aspects of his or her life, the addict may be able to make completely sane and rational decisions, but with regard to the focus of their addiction they are completely crazy. Each time a decision regarding their drug of choice comes up, their disease will assert itself with overwhelming influence such that the alcoholic in the moment of sitting down at the bar actually believes that it is a good idea, or the only idea. This feels just as true to an addict as a hallucination appears completely real to a schizophrenic. When our consciousness is under the influence of insanity that influence is complete. At that point it is not a matter of willpower or increased conviction. When left in the isolation of ourselves, we are at the service of the addiction.

This is why the first step is so difficult and so important. The addict must come to know deeply that he or she is an addict. They must come to recognize the voice of their addiction in their own consciousness, and when they hear it they must have a clear, well-defined, practiced plan about what to do. That plan must contain elements that reach out beyond themselves. At first it simply can be reaching out to another individual, but time and experience has proven that ultimately this reaching out must involve a power beyond. That, is in order to experience sustained recovery, reaching out must be to a power beyond the physical realm. Repeated relapsing among those who do not make this connection beyond the physical supports this knowledge. And with this knowledge, it is reasonable to believe that addiction is not just one of the most common diseases, it is not just one of the most deadly, it is the prototype of spiritual disease. Our denial of consciousness in envisioning is also a spiritual disease. It is not a coincidence that we are now, in exactly this time in history, challenged with our increasing awareness of this prototype of spiritual disease.

For a pneumonia, I can administer antibiotics, and with a reasonably intact immune system the patient will get well.[14] No expansion of awareness or other change in the patient's outlook is required. But, presented with the disease of alcoholism, I can predict that if the alcoholic's awareness does not expand to include the spiritual awareness of the connection between all things, i.e. coincidence, and a connection to a power beyond, that person will relapse again and again until consumed by the disease. There is nothing I can do to force this realization on the alcoholic. Nothing I can say or do will hasten this moment of realization. Not even escorting a smoker to the pulmonary cancer ward to view the end stages of smoking addiction affects the cigarette-addicted. Not even when a drinking companion dies of liver failure does the alcoholic accept that it will be the same for him. Yet there is a moment that comes in the course of addictive disease when change can be made. It occurs with the feeling represented in the slogan; 'sick and tired of being sick and tired.' It is when spirit reaches through denial in a moment that the ego is consumed with hopelessness. Later the recovering addict will recount a story of realization that there was more in the world than the addiction. These are their moments of coincidence. Listening to classically addicted individuals, I see no essential difference in their situation and ours. Awakening to consciousness in envisioning is no different from awakening from any other addiction.

---

[14] Leaving aside the issues of antibiotic resistant bacteria that are now developing.

It may seem strange to mention a disease like addiction in the context of a spiritual art of the present moment, such as the art of conscious envisioning. And yet, in our desire to awaken we must come an understanding of what we are awakening from. This chapter is titled 'Whatever It Takes.' If you want the truth of what it takes to awaken into consciousness, this is what it takes. The first chapter of this book is devoted to helping you understand how to know if you are ready. This second chapter is about choice. Just because you are ready to awaken does not mean that you will choose to do so. To become conscious in envisioning is no small project. To be able to sense the fabric of spiritual potentials and choose to support one and not another is a high art. It is not surprising that it touches on sensitive areas. When I began my own association with the disease of addiction I was uncomfortable applying the diagnosis to myself. *Every addict is the same in this.* The thought that I might have something to learn was simply not something I wanted to hear. I really enjoyed thinking of myself as healthy and unaffected. I made judgments about this in every second. In short *I enjoyed my state of denial*, just like every other addict.

As with the bow drill, where I have said that from the perspective of the teacher it is obvious to me that the spirit of the Earth is involved and baits the student by giving fire to some easily in the beginning and then demanding more, so it is with envisioning. We are given some early comforts along this path as if power beyond is pushing against our denial. If we choose to go beyond the relaxation available through breath and mindfulness, or available in the comfort of connecting with nature, or beyond the balance and rhythm of Hatha Yoga or the initial learning of Tai Chi or any of the other approach routes, if we actually we choose to pursue conscious envisioning, what comes next is not soft or comfortable. Before the next fire is given to us we will need to feel the bite of the cold and know our need. The next steps will weed out the feint of heart, the easily distracted, and those who aren't ready. There are no voyeurs beyond this step. Everyone you meet on this path will be seeking with all their might to awaken into a life that is magical, a life where the limits are removed, a life so rich in its meaning and depth that it can never end.

Bringing It Home

I am often asked if I think everyone can reach the level of capacity in envisioning that is needed for real change. I can only respond that they *can* but I do not know if they will choose to. Human beings are fascinating, gorgeous, locations of contradiction within the field of spirit. We constantly state one thing and do another. We do this even on the most obvious physical levels. One day we feel strongly about something and the next we aren't so sure. It is simply part of our human experience. There is nothing to be judged as good or bad. I have had times when envisioning flowed with ease and times when I am so confused I don't know if I am speaking a language at all let alone one the universe understands. An individual is neither strong nor weak, neither gifted nor ordinary. We are all completely unique, non-comparable elements of a unity. Understanding envisioning requires laying aside old beliefs with which we have become comfortable. It requires trying on new ideas and the willingness to experience differently. This can be felt as difficulty, as challenge, or simply as a choice.

I have a friend who once gave his four and six year old sons painting supplies and canvases. He encouraged them to get wild and do whatever they wanted. Then he came back and chose two out of dozens of canvases. He hung these in his office and they were admired by many and were called art. He would then ask, who was the artist? Was it his kids playing, or himself who was conscious of his process? It offends our sensibilities to say that the kids were not artists, that my friend was just using them to create art. The same experiment has been done with monkeys and even more random mechanisms. Perhaps we can understand that in unconscious envisioning we are participating in the art of something beyond ourselves, or perhaps it may be called the art of the collective unconsciousness. With expanding consciousness we are being asked if we want to raise our level of participation. We are the kids, growing up. We are now concerned about where and how to splash the paint. We are coming into our own as artists. It is possible that we may discover that we were better unconscious artists than we will be conscious artists for awhile.

Sometimes when I am asking a patient about their health they tell me that they think they are taking "good care of themselves." They then proceed to list the things they are doing that may include regular exercise, not eating red meat too often, limiting their exposure to fast foods and snacks and perhaps even taking some vitamins or supplements. Some of them may then add what they think of as their "last remaining vice," saying, "I have to have something." I often feel the undercurrent of these comments is: "I'm doing everything I can *but*"... and there is a residue of something that is fearful. Women tend to be more comfortable feeling this directly while men are more apt to express it in a joke or by either not wanting to take their medications or stopping them without consultation. This is a delicate point in the interview and the safest course is to steer away from or retreat into a more purely scientific mode. If I challenge men or women on their need for that last vice before they are ready to let it go there can be a confrontational reaction; none the less this sometimes may be the beginning of actual healing.

In waking up into conscious envisioning there is no room for the last vice because it is not what we think it is. It is not simply a habit or a pleasure. There is no such thing as a 'vice' really. In regard to personal health it is a symbol of resistance to doing absolutely whatever it takes to be healthy. It is a symbol because it is what you have chosen in order to continue to act in a way, you yourself, think you should not. As you choose to awaken, it will become clear that whatever you thought of as your last hold-out position, it was simply the last one you were aware of at that time. As you continue to make the choice to awaken, there will be a long list of 'hold-our positions' littering your back trail. Each time, you will be presented with the same question. Are you willing... to do whatever it takes... again?

In response to a frustrated Tom Brown Jr Grandfather Stalking Wolf was fond of saying:

"What is it that you are refusing to give up today grandson?"

Outside of the emergency medical environment I have become known as an 'alternative or holistic physician' and with this dubious title comes the assumption that I know everything, or at least something, about herbs and dietary supplements, or acupuncture, or homeopathy... and that my practice is based on them. I explain to my patients that what alternative means to me is that they are in charge. I tell my patients that no matter how smart I am or how much schooling I have I will never know as much about them as they do, because they are living their situation. The most I can do is know *about* their situation. Thus, I see myself truly as a trainer, an advisor, an information source, a witness, a provider of feedback, an encourager, and a prod. I am whatever I have to be to help them to do what *they* have chosen. The one thing I cannot do is to make their choice for them. While I may have some information about herbs, and supplements, acupuncture, homeopathy, and the more esoteric levels of human interaction, it is just information. I feel that my real role is helping each individual to find their own instincts, to find their own source of knowing what is right for them. What I am is accepting of them.

What is happening behind the scene, in the place where envisioning occurs, is that I am acknowledging that we are both individual systems of awareness. Both of us carry two sets of knowledge, that set of which we are aware and the set that we are blocking. In my role as trainer and advisor I use my awareness to hold an opening for them to see that which they are blocking. I am accepting them in their current state of awareness, but perceiving them as a being in complete awareness. Though I may perceive their system of illness I do not hold it as their reality. Instead, I hold as real the wholeness of their reality beyond their blocks. With the perspective of my separateness from them it is easier to see their blocks than my own. I acknowledge that this may be the gift and entire purpose of separateness, so even while I am in this process of observing the other person, I remain aware that I also am a system of awareness in evolution. Each perception of the patient holds toward me is a gift for which I am grateful.

Denial And Willingness

Denial is the mother of all addictions. By this I mean that when we find bacteria in the lung we can apply our diagnostic label, pneumonia, indicating that we can predict a typical course of events, one if treatment is begun and one if not. And, when we find denial in a system of awareness we can make our diagnosis of addiction, and reliably predict the typical course of events, one if treatment is accepted and one if not. The depth and completeness of denial is hard to fully comprehend until you have awakened from its grip. Just as with the disease of pneumonia, occasionally a cure can come about spontaneously, but this is rare with addiction. Much more often the disease will relapse and worsen unless specific treatment is accepted. In the case of the disease of addiction the treatment is a process. The most painful moments of this process are at the very beginning when the addict begins to suspect the truth. With regard to envisioning, these moments are heralded by attention to coincidence and the suspicion that something more than random events is occurring. At that point we are ready to look deeply but still don't suspect the actual depth of the change we are contemplating. When we get a glimmer of the truth, it is scary. The possibilities are too vast, too confronting. Sleeping in denial suddenly seems not so bad. It is like a Saturday morning lying in a warm bed having stayed in half slumber so long that you can remain no longer. When you throw off the covers you find that it is cold; next comes the clear instinct to climb back in where it is warm and safe. The problem is you are awakening now. Staying in bed isn't fun anymore.

This is why it is hard to discuss addiction of any sort with those who are about to awaken. The power of denial has been built within us over many millions of years. We have had to live through times when persecution was the norm. It is not so long ago that women and children were treated as a man's possessions. Before that, times of famine, times when our mothers were taken by animals, times were so brutal that denial truly was a survival mechanism for combating despair. Human beings have risen to the top of the food chain not because of strength or endurance but because of our adaptability. Denial has been a big part of that ability during the bad times. Now, we are in a different time. Each of us individually and all of us collectively are facing an even greater challenge to our adaptability. Are we adaptable enough to wake up? On the individual level the challenge appears in the form of our health, our relationships, our plans and our dreams. On the collective level it appears as skyrocketing health care costs, an epidemic of drug addiction, war, terrorism, AIDS, bird flu, and ecological turmoil, but it is the same challenge. To act on one level is to reflect on the other. If we accept this challenge we will learn that the separation of ourselves from all else is only an illusion. We may, by awakening into conscious envisioning, have the experience of healing the outer by healing the inner. But will we? This is the choice. Getting out of bed and enduring the cold is a choice. The essential ingredient is willingness. Do you want it enough to be willing to do whatever it takes?

Willingness is what is required to see through, or more actually to be released from, denial. It will take a process to undo this powerful mechanism, but until we become willing there can be no release from denial or recovery from the disease of addiction. For most addicts, the stimulus for willingness is that their situation gets so intolerable that they see their choices limited to two: become willing to surrender their addiction or to die. This is what addicts call hitting bottom. For addicts of all kinds this seems to be a common thread. Gamblers have to lose their last dollar. Crack addicts must lose everything and then steal or prostitute themselves often to the very brink of death. Many, in fact, do die of the disease of addiction. Ultimately, I am saying that all of us will die, of and in, addiction if we persist in our denial of awareness, believing in separation, until the very moment of our deaths.

One of the most meaningful coincidences that came into my life when I began my study of envisioning is that almost everyone I met and became close to was a substance addict. Most of these people were in various stages of recovery and my association with them led me to perceive a recovery of my own. My addiction was not with a substance but with control and was maintained by denying my own egocentric mode of perception. I was the sort of person who had opinions about everything and I liked to express them. I'm a smart guy. I have been to school a long time. Therefore, sometimes my opinions were informed and seemed to align with what the experts say. I thought this justified the frequent expressions of my opinion. However, I didn't just express my opinions I projected them with an air of control and judgment. The result was the enforcement of separation. I was seen as arrogant. At times it produced a situation that was unpleasant for me and in the end, it became downright unmanageable.

Recovery is not a state of perfection but a state of willingness. Opinions still rocket around in my head and I often offer them up occasionally. This book is an example of such an opinion. Each of us sees the world through our own personal view and we can express little else, but I look for the willingness to allow what I feel, think, and say to be guided by something beyond myself. It is this power beyond self that unlocks the door of denial. Beyond that door is where envisioning takes place. To be in conscious relationship with power beyond through conscious willingness allows the envisioning that comes from that relationship to be conscious as well. I look for the willingness to hold my beliefs lightly and for the willingness to let them go altogether when needed.

The willingness required in recovery is not a willingness to do anything specific. It is not an act of will or of doing an action, but of one of surrender, of undoing. This surrender is not a defeat but a victory. It is finally, to put down the burden of what has been exhausting you. This is what has, unknowingly, been keeping you from your goal. Thus, recovery is not a move into a state of perfect health or perfection of any kind but of finding of the willingness to do whatever it takes to be in relationship with power beyond.

This is the connection between recovery from classical addiction and awakening to conscious envisioning. Both exist as addictions of focused attention that can be broken in relationship to power beyond self. We need not actually choose to *be* in relationship with power beyond. The fact that this relationship exists is beyond our purview. We did not create the world in which we live nor did we create ourselves. We do have a hand in creating what happens and how. We can choose to become conscious of ourselves and of our relationship. The choice that guides whether an individual will become conscious of envisioning lies in their willingness to surrender an egocentric worldly view. Thus, we may become aware of placing our attention exclusively in service of the ego. We may instead choose to become conscious in our relationship with power beyond.

Historically there has been a tendency to personify, or make human, our ideas of power beyond. We love to argue and even foment wars over this issue. But, it is not a power *beside* self nor is it a *partnership*. It is not a relationship of *equals*. All these notions are ideas involving "hierarchy." The ideas that one is better than, worse than, larger than, smaller than, or in some relationship *via* an attribute of comparison, are constructs of the human ego. Our exclusive attention to these judgments is the addiction of attention that the ego depends upon. All aspects of relationship with power beyond are *beyond* comparisons of any kind. Power beyond self is truly beyond. It is beyond all the constructs in which the self exists.[15] These constructs include all aspects of the world as described by our ego, all our relationships, our needs, our desires, even beyond our comfortable concepts of space and time.[16]

---

[15] The definition of self will eventually come under scrutiny later in the study of envisioning. The statement that the only thing an individual can change is *self* remains true in envisioning. However, the concept of self may change.

[16] At this point you may be able to appreciate the difficulty in choosing the word that must go between the words *power* and *self*. Twelve Step Programs use the words *higher than*. Other possible words might be greater than or better than but you see that these are comparison words. Personally I was fond of *power not self* since the notion that this power is not yourself is the essential element when viewed from the perspective of a self, defined by ego, which is the most common state. But, this leaves the problem that once ego is seen and placed in its proper perspective the word *not* becomes problematic. So, after many discussions with othres I ended up with the word "beyond." I am hoping that the combination "power beyond," gives the feeling of expansion

In order to consciously envision, the mind must surrender its urge for control. This urge may be examined in the psychological realm. We are all somewhat familiar with the concept of trying to control others or trying to control our work or our family environment. We must go even deeper now. Our mind must accept the fact that the world it believes in is a self-construct and is not a substantial reality. That is, it is not a reality of substance, but simply a location for experience. If you want to awaken from the grip of that experience and enter into consciousness of your relationship with power beyond, then you must accept that the experience has become repetitive, out of control, and unmanageable by you. You must become willing to let that experience, and your control of it, go. Essentially, you must admit that it represents an addiction. The presence of this addiction to a certain experience is expressed through the conviction that things are the way they are, with nothing to do with you. The non-addicted reality is instead, that things are the way they are having absolutely everything to do with you. In our accustomed state, we would prefer to remain in denial of our own impact and we can. There is nothing easier. It will exhaust us into death but, each of us can go on just has we have, semi-conscious, addicted to what has been. All addicts want to feel better *and* keep their addiction. It is just not possible. To recover we will have to face the actuality of real change.

Addiction is the quintessential disease of our age. The drug trade, both illicit and pharmaceutical, is shaping the geopolitical landscape in a way that is perhaps only surpassed by oil. It can be said that our economy is completely addicted to oil. Within our society our addiction to food is seen with a huge rise in obesity, type II diabetes, hypertension, and the other attributes that are becoming known as Metabolic Syndrome, or Syndrome X. The judgment that addiction is bad, that those who are addicted are inferior or defective in character, must be

---

both of the possibilities of power and of the possibilities of self. Of course you may choose to use any words you wish.

examined and surrendered. This judgment serves only to separate us from awakening to the truth that we are all suffering from an addiction of attention. To know *about* envisioning is possible without this particular sacrifice of belief and without a redefinition of self. But in order to actually awaken into the field of existence where envisioning can be known consciously, this sacrifice and redefinition is required.

For any effort to become conscious in envisioning, all allegiance to the constructs of the mind obstruct the path.[17] In order to be surrendered the constructs of the mind must be seen clearly and they must be understood as unmanageable representations of disease. Without doing so, we simply will resist surrendering what we think is still working for us. All aspects of what is held as real by the mind seem *real* precisely because these aspects are held closer to our awareness than our relationship to power beyond. This is what must be surrendered. When the relationship to power beyond self is held closer than all that came before, then the stage will be set for our recovery and for awakening to conscious envisioning. Then our lack of willingness to surrender what our minds held as real will be seen as exactly similar to an alcoholic's lack of willingness to see his drinking as the problem. It is the same as the needle addict's craving, the gamblers need, or a codependent's love for the feeling of enmeshment. To recover from any addiction, the first step is always the same. The model is not obscure. We must come to admit that we are powerless over our creation and that our lives have become unmanageable.

Strong stuff, hey? You think I'm beating it to death? I'd be willing to bet you are still questioning it. There have got to be other ways to skin this cat! Your life isn't all that bad. It

---

[17] Lesson #1 Nothing I see as it is now. #2 I have given everything I see ... all the meaning it has for me. A Course in Miracles Foundstion for Inner Peace 1992, Workbook for Students page # 15

certainly isn't *unmanageable* is it? This addiction / recovery stuff, it is probably all right for some people, certainly the alcoholics and the drug addicts, but isn't it a bit of a stretch to apply it to everyone?

Have you had any friends who are alcoholics? Drug addicts? Have you ever talked to them when they are using? Are you suffering, or have you suffered in a classic addiction? Smoking? Fast food? I believe I have spoken, either as a physician or as a friend, to hundreds of classic addicts of one kind or another and I can tell you from experience that these are exactly the same thoughts they have. They are the thoughts produced by, and projected by, active addictive disease. "I will find another way." "It is not that bad." "I will never be like them." "I'm still OK! Damn it!"

Many of my addict friends who have made it to a genuine recovery from their substance of choice have heard me say that a part of me (certainly not all of me) envies them their disease because in their lives, the symbol of unmanageability is clear. For them it is clearly a do or die situation. For the rest of us including codependents and folks who are just "normal" it is not so clear.[18] We must pursue our own recoveries with equal vigor but with less concrete consequences. We can, and most of us will, choose not to surrender our current beliefs. Most of us will go to our graves having unconsciously envisioned all our days.

An argument can be made that the events of recent ecological and geopolitical history from antibiotic resistant

---

[18] I have a friend who believes that someone you think of as "normal" is just someone you don't know very well. This seems more and more accurate to me.

bacteria, to terrorism, from Dutch Elm disease and tsunami's to global warming are just coincidental manifestations of the fact that the world we are living through our collective envisioning has become unmanageable. We could choose to surrender the sovereignty of our egos now and allow power beyond into our individual and collective awareness just to see what happens. Our minds and our ego's are not going disappear. We may learn that they are not the source of our individuality but they will always remain one of our most valuable tools. Each of us has this choice to make. I have said why it is important and explained exactly what the choice is. It is to become willing to do *whatever it takes* to hold our relationship with power beyond closer to us than our relationship with the world as defined by our ego.

The Art Of Conscious Envisioning

Chapter 3

Climbing The Pyramid

Surrendering Value Judgment

> There are many parallels to the Twelve Steps of Alcoholics Anonymous s in this third chapter. I do not intend to rewrite the twelve-step program in any way, but it has been useful to me. Each of us comes to understanding in our own way. Any written device is only a guide, this

The first step is accepting the diagnosis. Think of the diagnosis as "physically focused or restricted attention, " or "physically addicted attention," if this works for you. To restate once again because it truly is the hardest to understand, let alone do:

We have to admit that when we hold the physical world and all it contains closer to us than our inner connection to power beyond (whatever that is in our own personal understanding), we are trapped in our self defined world which may include disease, distrust, negative thoughts, negative experiences, even positive experiences... whatever.

As long as we accept the belief that these things are more real than our connection to power beyond nothing but the surface details of our lives can consciously change. If we do decide to allow our connection to power beyond to become closer to us than anything else, look out for the miracles, because the possibilities will become immeasurable.

Once we decide to move in this direction, the direction toward building our conscious envisioning, the next question is how do we go about it. That is what these next pages are about. I'm not writing a book *about* how it might be done, this is a handbook for the experience of doing it. I mentioned that during my early, church-related experiences in relationship to spirit I was told to believe first and trust that the reasons would become known later. I said this didn't work for me, but later, through the pathway of studying wilderness awareness, I found a method, experience first, that led me back to things of spirit. While I would love to have you all out in the wilderness for a month or so for this experience, it seems impractical.[19]

With breath training our attention is lured away from the mind and ego toward the body. This is done with pure diaphragmatic breath because the diaphragm is wired to both the conscious nervous system (the seat of the ego) and the unconscious system (something that is not directly controlled by the ego). After some experience with breath training we begin mindfulness next, which brings us into awareness of the observer. This is in the direction of spirit because that is really the only direction we can go. Attention is held either by ego or by spirit or perhaps by some uncontrolled mixture of the two creating possibly even insanity. The discovery of the observer delivers us to a place where we can begin the current phase of our journey. Through use of the observer we can begin cultivating balance of mind, body and spirit. This is the journey I am calling climbing the pyramid. Within the experience of the observer there is the seed of this journey. We begin to recognize that there might be something beyond ourselves. This power beyond is in the direction the observer has moved

---

[19] I will note however, that the resistance that I often hear regarding going into wilderness parallels exactly the unconscious resistance to accepting powerlessness in the face of unconscious envisioning. Similarly to what often happens when I am able to eventually coax an individual out in to pure wilderness they find that it is easier and more magical than they had imagined. The experience on the other side of acceptance is rarely, if ever, as bad as the ego tells.

away from the ego. There is the impression that if we could continue to move in that direction we could come to know something new. Willingness, though it is what we have been cultivating, doesn't actually tell us what to do.

Once we decide to, the actual mechanism of surrendering to a power beyond is simple. Determine when you are making "value judgments" and give that function over to power beyond. This is an act of surrender because there is an element of compulsion. To reach into our humanity into the possible experience of being human we must surrender the control of our ego and its habit of value judging. Thus, we surrender because we have to. If we do not, the pathway to conscious envisioning will remain closed. This act is not simply a release of control to some nebulous entity. It is surrender to a specific power with which you have a relationship. "To surrender" takes more than "to release." To surrender is not a trivial act. It is one that is done only with great consideration and consequence. To surrender to one's enemy may feel like a defeat. If your version of power beyond is a vengeful one, then your surrender may in fact be a defeat. In that case it might be better to maintain the illusion of ego control until your construct of vengeance can be put aside. When a two year old finally surrenders to sleep after hours of being rocked in his parent's arms, there is no defeat. Surrendering to a version of power beyond that is pure love is not defeat. It is victory. [20]

A value judgment is anything you think you know where you are making a decision about the essential nature or character of something. Most often the use some conjugation of the word to be, thus they are *being* statements. Pay particular

---

[20] In Twelve Step programs there is a tradition of sponsorship. An individual is asked to surrender decision making to a sponsor first. This makes sense because in the case of classic addiction a vengeful version of power beyond is common in the beginning. Though they may not appear so in an intoxicated state, most classic addicts are much more self-judgmental than are non-classically-addicted individuals. Until recovery is underway it may be best to allow another individual to become power beyond. No separate person is generally as vengeful as the addict is toward him or her self.

attention to thoughts that begin with the words I am, he is, she is, or that is, and then are *not* followed by an action, like 'going to the store' but a description, like 'smart, dumb, creative, poor.' These *being* statements are judgments that masquerade as descriptions. They are not necessarily judgments of good or bad, but of specifying the quality or exact nature of an entity. To say someone is creative is neither good nor bad but it is assigning a value label. It is a placing of our awareness into the confines of a category. This is the addiction of attention in action. Rather than allowing the pure being of an object or person to simply radiate from it, our ego assigns a value, a definition, to it.[21] We then no longer need to consult with anything beyond ourselves to recognize that object or person. We may even stop being *with*, or *in* the experience of the actual being and instead we will be in relationship to our assigned value. Essentially, we become in relationship with our selves only having become trapped by the egocentric values of our focused attention.

Many value statements are "relative" value statements. The statement "she is beautiful" is not a pure description such as "she has long hair." It is more often a judgment that implies a relative value. These judgments rarely come in simple form. They are usually layered or comparative, relative, or complex (more than one meaning at a time) such as, "she is more beautiful than I am." "He is smart therefore he is smarter than me, or [insert name]". "He was able to solve that problem eloquently," is almost a description but "eloquent" has some overtones of a value. "He is smart," is a clear value judgment. "He solved that problem in three minutes," is simply descriptive. In order to surrender to a power beyond, consider leaving anything that is assigning a *value* up to that power. Our egos love value judgments and will camouflage their nature from us naturally because this is the mechanism of the ego's function. When enough values are assigned via the ego's work

---

[21] In mathematics a variable is given a 'value' when it is assigned a quantity, a number.

what is gained is that the world can be navigated via predictable assumptions. What is lost, however is the mystery and the magic.

We can use the observer, triggered by diaphragmatic breath, to examine value judging. Simply bring the disciplines of mindfulness and breath into our daily affairs with the purpose of examining our thoughts for the presence of value judgments. For myself, and for most people I have spoken with, this doesn't seem like an easy task. We are accustomed to going through our daily affairs with no underlying project. Change does not come without effort. The process responds to practice and gets easier as we go. We just need to start and it is good to have a specific plan. We have studied breath and mindfulness. We know what they are. Now we get to use them. Do they have to be in the forefront of your mind at all times? No. This is not possible. But, with just a little practice when you do make an obvious value judgment you will begin to notice. Rather than becoming self-judgmental you may continue to observe and gradually, without reinforcement, value judging will loose its control over your thoughts and actions.

Think of the experience like this. Imagine you are standing at the bottom of a pyramid. The sides are not smooth. Each layer creates a step. It is true that the steps are high climbing them is possible. First you must put one foot up on the step. Then you gradually shift your balance to that foot. When you are balanced you stand up and bring your other foot up. Now you are standing on the first step. It was a process. You went through a transition and at the end you solidified your balance at the higher level.

Finding the observer and cultivating willingness is the act of bringing up that first foot. By having that experience your awareness changes. The way you think will be displayed to you and be less unconscious. Now, if you are willing, I suggest an experiment: observe your thoughts for value judgments and ask yourself if they are really required. I suggest that you stop making them and see what happens. That is the act of shifting your balance and beginning to stand up. When you have fully surrendered value judgment you will be standing. Examples of Value Judgments:

1) There are many ways that value judgments appear in our lives. Many of them are complicated, interpersonal and subtle. While they eventually would be surrendered just as all value judgments need to be, it is not necessary to begin with the more difficult ones. The surrender of simple value judgments is just as powerful and a clearer place to begin. There was a time, for example, when I was very afraid of the cold. I wasn't clear for many years that I was actually afraid. I just thought the cold was uncomfortable and that I didn't like it. Though there were times when this was inconvenient for me, there was also a lot of support for my feelings. A lot of other people were also uncomfortable with the cold.

As I have said, much of my personal path toward conscious envisioning has been in exploring my relationship with nature and this is one of those examples. I had come to a place in my study where I was able frequently, but not always, to choose to see wholeness and beauty in my surroundings first, rather than seeing the specifics. On this day I was with some others camping and we had gone to a nearby river to bathe. We were not so much in a group as arriving and leaving at our own pace. I had arrived first and was crouching at the edge of the water looking in. It was not particularly clear, but I could see in. Mostly I was just looking at the water and feeling it rushing by. I ran my hand lightly over its surface to feel the energy of its movement.

At that time some of the others arrived and someone asked me if it was cold. Looking up I realized I hadn't thought about it. In fact, I had already removed my shirt before becoming interested in looking at the water. I hadn't really been aware of the temperature for some time, but in looking up at the others I noticed that it had started snowing. The flakes were huge and lazy. I said, yes it was cold, but in that moment I realized that I was using the word for the first time as a pure description. The water was simply cold, not *too* cold, not *uncomfortably* cold, not *fearfully* cold.

I stood up to continue my intention of bathing, and as I undressed I watched the snowflakes as they drifted down and gave themselves to the rushing water. As I stepped into the water I remained in that place of non-judgment, and although my breath caught when I ducked my head under, it was just a reaction of my body to the feeling of the water. I found that as I experienced the sensations without value judgment my body responded naturally. In a few moments, though I could still feel the rushing cold of the water against my skin, my body had become noticeably warm and comfortable.

I looked at the others who were crouching at the bank of the river laughing and joking about how it was too cold to really wash. They were having their experience and I was having mine. I felt a pathway of thought leading to the formation of a value judgment concerning the comparison of our experiences and then I felt the separation that judgment would create. A smile formed on my face as I chose to watch them and share in their experience without leaving my own.

As I climbed back on the bank we talked and I laughed with them. I felt invigorated. Someone asked if I wasn't "freezing." And I just said "no," that I was warm. Toweling off I could feel the air and the snowflakes touching me. As I got back into my clothes I felt their warmth and was grateful for it. What could have been at best, forcing myself to go through a fearful experience because of my commitment to get clean in the middle of the camping trip, had become a grand exploration of pure experience[22].

Climbing the trail back up to camp a man I didn't know very well said to me "good job," and somehow I knew that he had understood my experience. Perhaps he had surrendered that particular value judgment himself or perhaps he would next time. I didn't question it. Instead I shared with him a connection through the contact of our eyes that I have remembered ever since.

This is the magic, for me, of learning through my relationship with nature. The river had no agenda to be comfortable or uncomfortable. It simply was, and didn't respond to my judgment or simple description. I knew, and know this through all the levels of my being, mind, body and spirit. Whatever I chose to experience was totally up to me. If something such as the value of coldness in a fast flowing

---

[22] See the definition of 'Pure' as addressed later in this chapter.

river in the snow can be surrendered, and with it the experience that value would generate, and if a new, unfettered, relationship can come to birth in relationship with spirit then, truly, there is no limit.

2) I have witnessed another way that many of my patients make a subtle but very powerful value judgment. When a person comes in with, say, a painful swollen ankle, knee or wrist very often they will use the words "*the* ankle hurts". It may sound ordinary, trivial, but realize that the use of the impersonal pronoun "the" is in this case, a powerful value judgment. The offending extremity is no longer fit to be owned. The tragedy is that in disowning through this subtle value judgment the person also disavows all connection to the extremity and thus any conscious capacity to heal.

Thanks to the goodness of our collective envisioning these individuals do usually come to unconscious healing in time.

Of course there are many hurtful and obvious ways in which we apply value judgments to ourselves by allowing ongoing self-critical buzz of words in the backs of our minds. We allow these habits of the mind to continue because we feel powerless to stop them. They are self-destructive in the extreme because we do not focus our attention on them. This is not a surprise, but it is a problem. We are like the addicts who, every time they light up, or drink, or use, admonish themselves that they have to quit. Which is worse: the direct effect of the addiction on the body or the self-critical and shaming value judgments?

It is also true that all value judgments are not negative. We all know that most are, but in surrendering value judging we are not being selective. Allowing our power beyond to make *all* the value judgments is the point. In return, through surrender to a loving power, we will find more positive feedback than we would ever previously have allowed ourselves.

Marshall B. Rosenberg has described this material in his book "Nonviolent Communication." Though he is not describing these concepts in relationship to addiction or surrender, and, though he is generally referring to communication with others while I am more concerned with communication inside the self, his discussion of value judgments and how they affect us is easy to read and understand. He describes many experiences where he teaches non-value-judging communication to individuals and groups and the results are consistent. Rigid structures of assumption and denial drop away and change occurs. The power described in his work has been born out in difficult negotiations around the world. Perhaps he doesn't use the words "addiction" or "denial" because they are such loaded words, but for this reason precisely, I am using them. When we have removed the flavor of value judgment from the words "addiction" and "denial" then we will have the potential not just to communicate nonviolently but to envision consciously.

When we have surrendered value judgment to our personal version of power beyond, all meanings that were once assigned by our ego consciousness will now be communicated through our relationship with power beyond. We will begin to see that what we thought the world meant to us is not what it actually means. We will have taken our next step toward living a magical life, a life where our soul is at home and our minds can find, at long last, rest.

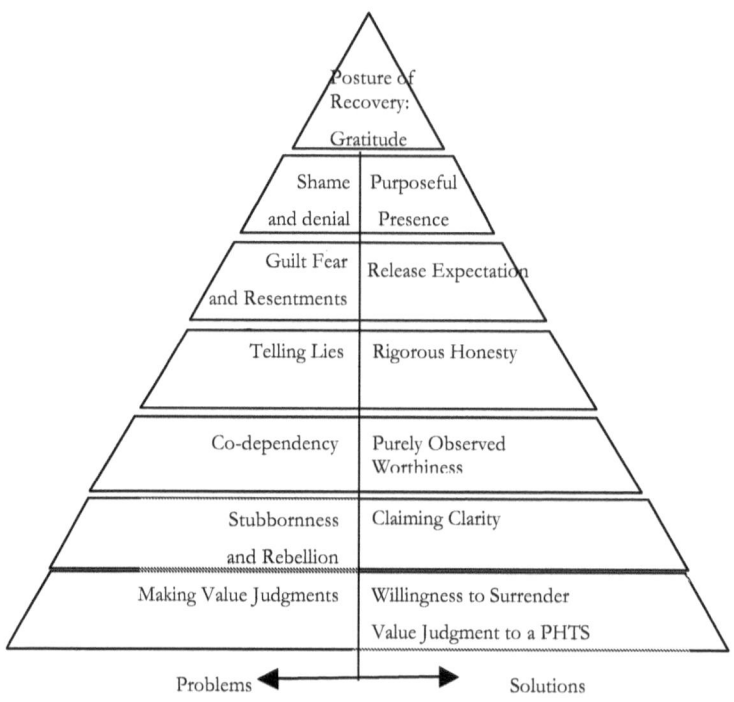

I use this diagram to help communicate the process of awakening. We will go through each step in turn. With the tools and experiences of Pure Diaphragmatic Breath and

Mindfulness, we have brought ourselves to a place where we can begin to step up onto the first layer of surrendering value judgment. This first step is the largest step. It is the foundation for everything above. Once the foundation is laid, successive steps are easier and easier. Not only is this true because the first step is the largest but because it is the first time you have experienced this sort of climbing in the realm of awareness. Surrendering value judgments to power beyond self is the first, the hardest and the most important step. It is the step that releases your awareness to new sights and possibilities. Once that is accomplished, even for a few moments, you can access a new realm. In this realm your version of power beyond, rather than ego, is allowed to inform your eyes and ears. This is a realm of *Clarity*. Coming to surrender value judgment is to balance on the first step.

Now we can see the second step. Seeking clarity is the second step. Clarity is not a function of the mind. It is a gift you receive through surrendering value judgment to a power beyond. In normal consciousness, or what most of us think of as normal, we see the world through a lens that has been constructed by our ego. That is the mechanism of our brain. We establish millions of value judgments that allow us to function in the world as we do. I like peas. Jane doesn't like green beans. Mommy loves me. Strangers are bad. This function of the brain is not a bad thing. If we had no ego, no mechanism of the mind, we would still be as newborns looking out on a world completely unfiltered, unknown, and strange. But, having accomplished the task of the ego, our souls may now be hungering for more balance in our awareness. This is the instinct that draws our attention to the meaning behind coincidence. Co-incidence is, basically, that event or item that doesn't fit into what we expected. It is something that comes to our attention that jars our awareness out of its habitual pattern. Often, it is the juxtaposition of an event with an uncommon awareness that preceded it. Ego consciousness will stubbornly suggest that we ignore this event, feeling, or item. Despite this a part of our consciousness that desires to awaken from the habits of the ego is attracted. If we continue to allow ego control over our attention we will allow the awareness to pass by, again. If the urge is sufficiently strong we might look further and wonder what this awareness of coincidence has to offer. The ego is a tool of perception. As a tool it helps us in our interpretation of the world but it is not our only tool.

What would happen if we put aside the lens of the ego, if we allowed our attention to roam freely through what it previously has seen and digested? What often happens is that fear appears. Sometimes just a little, if that is all that is needed, more, if more is required. The purpose of this fear is to redirect our wandering attention back to the control of the ego. It is the fear that *if* the ego does not control our attention, our awareness, then what will? Our ego warns us that beyond its control is chaos. It is like the maps before the days of Columbus and Magellan. "Beyond Here There Be Dragons." That is what the cartographers actually wrote on the best maps of the day. This was the state of the collective consciousness at the time. The courage of those sailors who decided to go beyond the known into the land of dragons is the same courage required to see the ego in its true light. The ego has served us well. We have solidified our awareness in the physical world. It has told us truly about this land that seems to be flat, but we are hungering for more information. There is some indication that those dragons might not be real. It is possible that beyond the ego's boundary there might actually be magic?

The magic beyond the ego is not dissimilar to the new land found by Columbus. The arena of awareness beyond the control of the ego is a new land indeed. The ego's fear that, if it is not in control, awareness will dissolve into nothingness is just a fear. Only when surrender takes place, only when the journey is actually taken, can this understanding be experienced. The fact remains that the world is round, and it was round, even before Columbus.[23] There is a power beyond the ego. There always has been and always will be. This power beyond is not of our creation. We are of its creation. This is why it doesn't matter how we think of it. It is what it is, regardless of our belief, our definitions, or our images. It only matters that we allow our ego's control to surrender to it. Only then will we know that power for what it is. Only then can our attention find the Clarity that is available when our vision is shifted from the lens of our ego to the lens of power beyond.

It is an artifact of the many attempts the ego has made to keep from surrendering control that we have so many constructs to explain power beyond to ourselves. How many

---

[23] I do realize that it is historically inaccurate to place this all at the foot of Columbus given that the Nordics had already been across the Atlantic, but Columbus and then Magellan are credited for this change of consciousness on a wide scale.

religions, symbols, and belief systems has humankind developed to interpret this veil without actually explaining it? There are as many as the average addict creates to rationalize his addiction. The choice is the same as the addict's. The only mechanism for actually walking through the veil without dying is to find the willingness to do it so. No matter what it takes.

This willingness to do whatever it takes is willingness to look to power beyond first in every situation. The ego still plays its role as pure observer but it must surrender the determination of what everything *means*, every value judgment, to power beyond. In past history we have many examples of what happens when an individuals holding a vengeful version of power beyond is willing to do whatever their ego's feels is necessary. The results have been horrific. Even now some people are willing to poison our water, commit acts of terrorism, subjugate others in acts of ego-guided allegiance to a vengeful versions of power beyond.

Conscious envisioning is not accessible through a vengeful version of power beyond. Not in my experience. The results of allegiance to vengeful gods is well known to human kind and they are events very much of the ego and the physical plane. What conscious envisioning requires is surrender of the ego's control. The mechanism for doing this is not performing a ritual or even behaving well. Religion as such has done a great deal to raise humankind out of barbarism and has generally been helpful for changing the overall state of behavior in civilized society, but to seek conscious envisioning is to look deeper, beyond the root of behavior, to the source of perception itself.

Attention to coincidence is a symbolic choice that we make. It represents our willingness to hold the lens of power beyond to our perceptive eye. This creates a crack in the ego's armor, the ego's absolute hold on our attention. Attention to the body through pure abdominal breath and to thought through mindfulness gives that crack room to grow. This brings us to the pyramid and the willingness to place our foot upon the first step. We are delivered to the place where we can choose to surrender making habitual value judgments. As we come to surrender value judgment and move from the ego we begin to experience that our prior understanding was an illusion to keep our consciousness imprisoned within what we thought we knew. Despite the fear projected by the ego, awareness does extend beyond its boundaries. With the dawning of this understanding we gain movement toward clarity. We move the weight of our experience up onto the second step. This is the willingness to accept that our relationship with power beyond self is our primary, our closest, relationship, and that our relationship with the world and all that is in it is secondary. Coming to this realization presents the second level of the pyramid. The climb goes on. Occasionally, we will fall back into value judging, and we will feel the stubbornness of our ego's hold, but having tasted clarity even once, most of us will not relinquish it again for long.

Knowing Clarity

We discuss in this section the blocks that each of us have that keep us from being conscious of the mechanism of Envisioning in our lives. The first block is accepting that we have been seeing the world in limited form, not as it really is. We see our decisions and our judgments about the world. These judgments are then cemented by our assigning a value to them. Next, we place the world and our connection to it in the prime position within our awareness. This makes the world seem ultra real to us and places its reality in a position above our own awareness of it. With our ego in control we become very stubborn that this is the actual case. The truth is our awareness of the world may actually come first and the presence of the world, second, but we reject this notion within our functioning reality. We do this in our modern times even while knowing that the basic laws we have formed to understand our world, i.e., quantum mechanics, state otherwise[24]. We do this by separating the basic, ultra small, particles of the world from our larger, experiential world even while acknowledging that one is based upon the other. In our day-to-day functioning awareness we simply overlook the connection. After all it works. Just like it always has.

What would it take to change our stubborn position? Perhaps we would have to come to a place where things working just as they always have is no longer good enough. This is the pain when the addict has reached bottom. Sometimes it takes a long time to reach this place. Another possibility is that we find an attractive alternative such as climbing the pyramid. In this case we would then have to judge ourselves worthy of attempting the climb. Often people are given a gift, like a moment of clarity, but do not know why this gift is coming to them. They are suspicious of it. They do not believe that this world is the kind of place where you may receive gifts for no reason. If they cannot recognize a reason for the gift within themselves, they will reject the gift. This is clearly the ego's handiwork, and it happens in an eye blink.

At this place in development, even though we have some experience of the first and second steps, our ability to surrender value judging still coms in momentary flashes at best. When we are faced with clarity the next notion that comes to most of us, certainly to me, is that we are not worthy of such a high level of awareness. The world as seen in clarity, through the lens of power beyond, is quite a bit more beautiful, more fantastic, more wondrous and magical than the world as seen through the lens of the ego. It is alluring but it is also unsettling, at least to the ego. Therefore, the rebound is sometimes extreme. You may choose to put conscious envisioning on hold for a while.

Like any addict who comes close to recovery but then judges himself not quite ready, it sometimes takes years and a

---

[24] The Heisenberg Uncertainty Principal suggests that awareness may determine the character of physical reality.

new depth of bottom before the realization of readiness surfaces again. Sometimes, with conscious envisioning, people think that the bottom doesn't matter because they are not dealing with "real" consequences such as a drunk driving ticket, being thrown in jail, an overdose, or losing loved ones, but this worries me. I have come to know that once a soul gets on the track of its true journey it doesn't give up lightly. Rather than feeling a smoothly assisting flow of coincidence a resisting ego's experience can become strikingly negative. The newly appreciated, but denied, awareness of coincidences can begin working pretty strongly against the desire of your ego to resist.

The apache and many schools of awareness believe in blindfold training. An exercise that Tom Brown Jr. uses in his school and that I have used with many people is called the Blind Drum Walk. Like many ideas of the Apache it is simple in method, but profound in depth. You set yourself up in the woods at a distance from someone who will be beating a drum. Put on a blindfold and walk toward the drum. The magic comes in when you add some requirement for commitment. For instance, the drum is a deep kettledrum with a very low note that curls around the landscape seeming to come from different directions. The drummer doesn't use any sort of regular rhythm and leaves pauses of several minutes between single notes. The drum is so far away that in the beginning it is hard to hear. The woods you choose are not open but rather a tangle of brush, bush, vines and trees. And, regardless of the weather, you are wearing only a bathing suit, no shoes.

This sort of blind drum walk takes four to five hours which allows time for your ego to go through all its phases of frustration, impatience, fear, demanding-ness, pleading, desperation until finally, if you have the commitment to leave the blindfold on, it has to surrender because it is absolutely exhausted. At that point something inside opens and a new experience begins. At that point The Blind Drum Walker stops without knowing why and reaches out to touch the tree trunk that an hour before would have been stumbled into. The Walker begins to turn with the landscape without knowing why, and blindfolded, never knows that a swamp was avoided. One time I ran a Blind Drum in an area that was open enough for me to video the Walkers. During the debriefing the next day, people were astounded at seeing themselves early compared to later in their walk. They commented on how it felt when they made this or that particular turn, and confirmed through a description of their feelings what before had only been suspected.

This is the beginning of the path toward a place in awareness the Apache call Nia-Cu pronounced (Ni-a-ku). I will relate it to a practical experience. Any of us who wander in the woods off the paths and become engrossed enough to lose track of time, may have been caught out late and found ourselves in areas too dark to see. In the place of awareness called Nia-Cu there is a light that does not come from the sky. It is a light that lets us know that we do truly live in a world of shadows. The light comes from around the things of the physical world. Tree trunks are seen in relief as if a silvery light is behind or within them. Layers of this light build up what is seen as depth. Wind curls within this light. The animals of the forest shine with it and their tracks hold it.

Walking within the light of Nia-Cu is as if in a place of quiet guided by the interaction of your own inner light and this light of the world. Focused thoughts have no place here and serve only to disturb the awareness fracturing it into unrecognizable patterns eventually extinguishing the awareness altogether. Destination and goals must be held lightly so as not to disturb the energy, or so passionately they create their own current, not as obligations or needs of the flesh, but in spirit. Destination must not become an ego desire but must remain within the relationship with power beyond. Within the Nia-Cu there is an interaction, a conversation with the world that is above the level of the ego's needs and fears. This is an area of awareness that challenges our feelings of worthiness. At first, any glimpse into this realm is often refuted out of hand by the ego. The feeling of unworthiness is so fast and deep that it goes unrecognized, but the awareness is extinguished, until the next time it happens. If we choose to walk a path toward awareness and if we are willing to do whatever it takes Nia-Cu is always there. It is not a place. It is energy in everyplace. It does not choose. We choose.

Even though I am presenting my ideas here with the help of the pyramid diagram in linear fashion, change is a "harmonic" function, as we discussed in chapter one. Though we are going through these steps as if they are isolated, they are actually occurring simultaneously, in an interactive harmonic. It is useful to bring each of them in turn to the consideration of our minds, but in reality there is only one shift, one experience. It is from the world as we see it now to the world as it actually is. I do not claim to tell you anything about that actual world, as it will appear to you, because it is for each of us to come to our own unique and individual awareness. Each of us has our own relationship with power beyond and it is through the lens of that relationship that clarity comes to each of us. This is the magic in each of us, and the magic that brings us all together into one.

The human brain is still vastly beyond our understanding. Even the word brain has undergone some changes in the way we understand it (*understanding*; a product of thought). Current thinking is that when we are born there are simply millions and millions of unused[25] interconnections among the neurons in brain matter. As we age we keep the neurons that we use and the others simply fade away. We know from experiments that, in older life, we seldom see things as they are but see them as we remember them to be. Our perception becomes habitual very quickly. It takes paying close attention to keep from falling into this trap. Have you noticed that vacationing in a new place always opens our awareness? Tom Brown calls it tourist consciousness. It is much more difficult to hide from someone new to his environment than from someone who is in a familiar place. This is the same reason that it is good to keep an infant's room lively with a changing variety of items and even better to take them outside. It is also why it is good not just to exercise our awareness in old pathways, but to open our awareness to new avenues as we get older.

I believe that the brain's adaptive ability is never lost, but we do have the choice whether we allow our habits to completely take over our awareness or to continue to seek new experience. The habitual road is paved with value judgments. Once we accept a value judgment our most habitual and unconscious neuronal pathway of perception regarding that element in our lives will remain the same. This is thought of as aging or as maturing, but it is not actually caused by the length of our temporal existence. It is a habit of thought in a mind

---

[25] I'm not so sure that these are really unused. I believe they may be used, just not in ways that we currently understand.

addicted to physical focus. It will take specific thought and intention coupled with surrender to release the habit, and the addiction. If we are able to do this new pathways can be built. Similar to recovering from a stroke, the brain reprograms. The more habitual pathways we allow to become imbedded, the more our vision will be clouded, until ultimately we do not really see at all, we just remember.

Often people say to me "but some habits are good". This *really is* contrary to what I am saying. No habits are good, none, nada, absolutely not a single one. I will agree that we will find situations where the same perception and response is repeatedly best, but to make that into a habit is to say that it is good to put it on autopilot. In the awareness we are building there is no autopilot. Habits are the home ground of ego consciousness. Imagine brushing your teeth in a new way, just slightly, every day, compared to assigning it a program and just letting it run while your mind and center of awareness floats off. I agree that brushing your teeth regularly is good. It is good not to forget it, but it is even better to do it consciously every time. The ego loves the habitual state. It is safe, non-threatening, un-challenging, and allows the ego to remain in uncontested control.

Clarity is our relationship with the world as it is seen through our connection to power beyond. Having surrendered value judgments we are no longer asking our minds what we previously thought. Instead, we are consulting a power beyond for each new understanding. Each time we do this our mind opens to a questioning state. The brain is asked to expand its possibilities. Our new understanding of the brain is that it does not just reside in our heads. The brain is a whole body organ. In turning value judgment over to power beyond we can begin to experience this. Our request for the brain to expand will lead us into new harmonics of awareness originating in our whole body brains.

Ultimately, each individual will formulate their own personal awareness of power beyond, but a few aspects bind us together. One is that power beyond is a power beyond our value judgment. This is what it takes to trigger our brains into expansion mode. And, this explains why a vengeful, or Value Judging, version of a power beyond does not result in conscious envisioning. Judgment always results in limiting possibilities.

Having surrendered value judging the experience of clarity will come. At first it will become present in flashes as you move in and out of surrender. Eventually through surrender, or whatever process you come to that brings the lens of power beyond to your primary perception thus producing clarity, you will begin to sustain the experience long enough to feel clarity distinctly. With this consciously known feeling of entering clarity we discover our reaction to it. This is a final value judging of our own worthiness. Are we worthy of remaining in clarity? Which then begs the next question, how does such worthiness come to us?

This is then the process of looking for the step beyond clarity. On this path finding the next step stabilizes the one just found. There is no resting point. It gets easier because growing in consciousness becomes more comfortable. Each new horizon is seen for its potential rather than as a trial. Each experience, pleasant or not, contains its lesson. Recovering from addicted attention is an ongoing process. We build our awareness gradually, climbing to the height of our personal best at the moment, always reaching for something new just beyond our capability. Each time we reach a new level we wonder if anything has happened at all, but subtly the world, as we know it, does change. Our "harmonic of awareness" grows with each time we surrender attention to power beyond. As we reach for the higher steps the lower ones become more sure. Our confidence in them grows even as our attention is drawn higher.

> I am reminded of a time I was watching my brother while he was rock climbing. We hadn't been together in a while and in my absence he had become very good. As I watched I realized he had developed a new technique.

To understand this you have to understand that in rock climbing, in the Eastern US at least, the level of difficulty of a particular climb is not steady or uniform the way it might be in a big crack climb out west. In the east the rock has more detail, more variation as you climb. This does not mean that any given route up a face is easier, just that there will be peaks of difficulty separated by relatively easier sections. Often even these easy sections are really difficult, but they do afford a relative rest from the hardest places.

As I watched my brother I saw that he climbed up into the cruxes, the most difficult areas, investigated, tried a move or two, and then immediately climbed down to a place of relative rest. Sometimes he might climb down as far as twenty feet. There he would think about his experience up higher. He would plan out the protection he was going to try and he would take a breather, of sorts. He was still hanging on to a vertical or over hung perch, but he would have found some combination of hooking his foot or elbow that was easier than anywhere else. Soon, he was on the move again up and down till he knew the territory he was traversing so well that it was taking less and less effort. Each time he reached the hardest part he was less tired. He knew what had worked and what hadn't, and eventually he would break through the crux and establish a new rest above.

At first his method seemed wrong to me. He was climbing the rock over and over again which seemed like it was more work than just going for it. But, he was getting up the rock without falling.

I came to think of my brother's rock climbing technique as Yo-Yo climbing (though I don't think I ever shared that with him). His technique came to mean a lot to me in my own climb through the stages of awareness. Each time I reached for a new level of awareness, rather than trying to hang until I expended all my effort in insecurity and fell, I began to climb back down to more familiar territory. If clarity felt difficult, rather than continuing to reach for it, I climbed down to begin working again with surrender. If I felt too stubborn to surrender I would retreat to examining coincidences again and ask myself if living in the flow was better than the turbulence I normally experienced. Before long I would feel stronger again and become curious about what it might be like if I really did surrender. Awareness of some value judgments I was making would come to me and I would feel able to reconsider them. Perhaps the earth actually would survive if I wasn't its judge and instead trusted that to something beyond myself. As I let go of judgment a little further, another hint of clarity would come to me, and, though worthiness was still an issue, I had been here before. It wasn't so bad this time…until, something else would happen and I would retreat to my rest again.

One day, using this technique of Yo-Yo climbing, I came to rest above the crux of my stubbornness, experiencing clarity comfortably, and even looking beyond. This time when I climbed down I didn't have to go all the way to find a rest. My world had changed and though I have been knocked down many times since, I know the route now. It doesn't take so long to climb up again.

There is one very reliable tool in the climb to higher awareness; that is the feeling gratitude.[26] This feeling more than any other seems to have the capacity to stabilize us at each point we reach. As we enjoy the new-ness, if we are grateful for what we have found we take it further into us. Gratitude also defeats the ego. What we are grateful for the ego cannot claim. We are grateful for what we have been given. Thus, something beyond us has done the giving. No matter what the struggle, an attitude of gratitude will point your awareness outside yourself. The feeling that there is nothing to be grateful for is a clear indication that the lens of the ego is operating. Sometimes, while in the grip of the ego's domain, it takes real effort to find something to feel grateful for. This happens when we have not climbed down to a safe rest, as my brother learned to do. We may fall either in exhaustion or because something has come along in our experience that knocks us to the bottom again. Either way, for me, sometimes all I can feel grateful for is that I do know, from my own experience, that if I choose to surrender I will come to clarity again. At times, even with this knowledge, it takes an amount of time living at the bottom to get ready to surrender again, but eventually I do. And, each time it is easier.

What makes the difference between making progress toward our goal and wandering in circles? That there is "method." The method I am describing is of an ordered series steps in which our awareness most efficiently and naturally grows. When we believe ourselves to be back at the beginning again, we really aren't because we have had experiences we can now remember. Climbing in awareness is as precarious as any rock climbing I have done. The sensation of having no firm ground, no rest, and no dependable balance is real. This is why we are either climbing or falling. Just trying to hang on in

---

[26] I think the word and concept "thankful" also works for now, but "gratitude" connects to a deeper meaning that we are coming to.

confusion or with effort does nothing but tire us out. Once we have been to the top and seen the capstone all this changes, but until then confusion and exhaustion are true aspects of the experience. Thus, knowing the next step to aim for is helpful. Having a direction laid out is helpful. In the end, all experience is uniquely individual, but companionship on the journey can be very helpful.

Purity

Standing on the second step in the experience of being worthy of clarity we are faced with the why of it. If we are not to fall from clarity, we have to accept that we really are worthy of it. How do we accomplish this? We need to find the next step. The concept of "purity" is next. Bringing purity to our mindfulness is placing our foot up. It takes some time to find this without help. I had the help of my teachers who had the help of theirs and so on. There is valuable assistance in this. Not "value" assigned by me, but valuable assistance through the experience of a lineage. We stand on the shoulders of our grandparents. We can value judge this assistance to death and start over each individually or we can try it out and see what the experience tells us.

What I learned from this linage is that the word "pure" is specific. It means: to be composed of one thing. One atom of another substance makes an entire ocean of water impure. One doubt makes a commitment impure. It is an impossibly high ideal for humankind to aspire to, but it is not necessary, nor even possible, to accomplish it by human means alone. We are, in our physical manifestation, creatures of the impure. The philosophic concept of Yin and Yang, the requirement of opposites for our experiential world to exist, is true to my experience. These elements are the bedrock of the collective unconscious envisioning. This world is, as the Apache say, a shadow world. Their term speaks to the impossibility of perfection in this world and the need therefore to surrender to a purer one. The Apache call the voice of clarity heard through pure surrender "inner-vision." [27]

It is important to understand that "purer" does not mean better than or worse than. It is not a value judgment. It is a description. If there is one atom of chlorine in the water, the water is somewhat more pure than if there are two atoms. We have a tendency to think of purer as higher, or more just. In fact, looking this word up in the dictionary will show that we use this word as a description *and* as a value judgment interchangeably. Sometimes we are speaking in hierarchy and sometimes we are not. I would like to use the word only in its descriptive meaning. Coming to know purity is a step on the path toward conscious envisioning. As such it is desired, something we aspire to, but it is not better than or worse than another way of being. Pure surrender means that no thought of resistance remains. This is why I personally prefer the word surrender to the word acceptance. I accept many things without agreeing with them. I accept that they are necessary or that in order to keep my job, they are necessary, but I have not surrendered my will to them. I continue to feel resistance despite my acceptance. In surrender there is none of this. Almost pure surrender means that there is still some doubt. That is natural, it is human, and it is a reflection of our world and our place in it. It is neither good nor bad, there is no value judgment, it is simply to be understood. But, the *concept* of purity is of absolute surrender, where not a shred of resistance remains. Perhaps this is not even human, as we normally understand it. Certainly, I have not found purity with out the help of power beyond.

When we reach for "pure surrender" our humanity will want to hold us back. This is the ego's hold. It is the hold of the world we have built together through unconscious collective envisioning. By ourselves it is impossible to reach "purity of surrender" or to experience "clarity:" perception completely

---

[27] As taught by T.B. Jr.

without taint of the Ego's function of value judgment. But, it is not necessary to do this by ourselves! These concepts become available to us only when we become willing to surrender. Our willingness comes and goes, but when it is present, when we hold our relationship with power beyond first, the gift we receive is the purification of clarity.

It is not a human purity but a purity of power beyond. It is as if we are stepping over a chasm. Left alone, the step is too large. There must be a hand on the other side helping. This is the experience of finding our connection to power beyond. This is why it must be *beyond*. It must be on the other side of the chasm created by the separation of ego perception and clarity. This is why nothing about an individual's notion of power beyond matters except that it is *beyond*, and that it is *forgiving* rather than *vengeful*. No one can be expected to truly reach out to a power that may vengefully let go at the crucial moment.

Our part is the willingness to reach out. Once contact is made we need only to surrender our attachment to the ego's side of the chiasm and to know that we are worthy of the journey to the other side.

During all the years of educating your mind, your teachers have been telling you that to *understand* is a function of the mind. This is the difference between understanding and clarity. Clarity is not of the mind but rather of your connection to power beyond. Clarity has nothing to do with having a *clear understanding*. Just as envisioning is not a product of thought but rather an experience of the partnership with power beyond, clarity is not a product of mental activity, but is the pure experience of our relationship to power beyond.

This experience becomes possible when we surrender our seat of awareness by ceasing to assign value judgments. In this way we release our pursuit of understanding by using the mind, choosing instead to open to clarity through our relationship to power beyond. Our job, our part, is to find the willingness to reach out our hand. We will be able to sustain this view of the world in purity, uncontaminated by the ego's habitual view, when we *know* that we are worthy of it. This *knowing* will come only through clarity itself, through accepting the vision of power beyond. Our worthiness is not dependent upon ourselves. We do not create ourselves. We simply participate in the choice of our experiences. We are not worthy because of our actions. We do not *earn* our worthiness. It is simply a fact of our relationship with power beyond. This is what I mean when I say that purity is impossible by human means alone. Isolated within ourselves we are dependent upon all the variables of the ego's world. This is not a fault of the ego. It is simply a fact. But, in uncompromised connection to power beyond, we may let go of what has been "understood" and reach out for clarity. This is not only possible it is the simple truth and function of our being.

The pursuit of purity is a life long pursuit. It is the direction in which we travel. It is a journey we may choose to take consciously or unconsciously, but it is our journey either way. The speed of our progress is up to us as determined by our level of conscious willingness. Again, I will repeat, because this is the most important understanding I can offer. What is it we are looking to purify? How does clarity come? How do we take our first steps? Purity follows clarity, which follows the connection that develops when we become willing to surrender value judgments and the ego's way of seeing the world. It does not require any specific understanding, fantastic vision, or ceremonial acknowledgment of power beyond. When we surrender we fall into the arms of power beyond naturally and without form or effort.

Think of it as if you are holding a cloudy lens in one hand and a clear lens in the other. If you first look through the cloudy lens everything will appear cloudy, even the clear lens. But, if you first look through the clear lens you will see clearly. You will even see the cloudiness of the lens in your other hand.

Your relationship with power beyond is the clear lens, and as long as you first look through the clear lens, you will see clearly. If you first look through the cloudy lens, that is, the ego's function of value judging, everything will look cloudy. If you deny your relationship with power beyond completely you will believe completely in the ego's perspective and lose sight of the other lens. At the height of the ego's reign the denial that we are even holding another lens becomes total, but it cannot remain that way. The ego does not live forever. If you choose to see that using the cloudy lens is creating unmanageability in your life. If you decide to surrender that unmanageability and do whatever it takes to change, if you let the hand fall that is holding the cloudy lens, then you have only one other option, only one other lens to use.[28] You are created an aware being. It is impossible for you to not focus that awareness somewhere. If you begin to learn to use the lens of power beyond, the world of clarity opens to you. If you understand your worthiness, even in this life, purity will come and your experience of the world will change.

When we are born we come from a place of total connection to power beyond. I have not personally found any utility in debating or defining the nature of that place. Some people believe firmly that before the egg and sperm there is nothing. I'm not arguing. I am describing the path to conscious envisioning. The notion of a physical place before birth where individuality exists hasn't been helpful to me. The notion that this place is defined spiritually *has* been helpful. If you want to think in terms of universal dark matter, or the compressed dimensions discussed in string theory, or another idea, it is all ok. I have explored these ideas too as my patients and friends have witnessed, but ultimately none of this has ever helped me progress toward the goal of conscious envisioning.

---

[28] It is true psychologically, that you can see yourself entirely through the eyes of another. In this way individuals may become enslaved to their thoughts about what they think others think. This though, is just a twist of the ego's camouflage. It is a projection onto others of intense self judgment and is just another way of using the ego's lens.

However, the thought that before our current physical life we were in a state of complete connection to power beyond, and that we were thus aware of all times and all things in the single, eternal, moment of the now, this thought has been helpful, because it allows me to understand the tool of the ego and see if for what it is. This helps me to surrender it willingly. It helps me conquer my fear that the ego is all there is. It helps me to reach out to power beyond.

It is possible to theorize that before birth, in total immersion with power beyond, there is/was no experience. There is no here or there no before or after. There is all, but there is no not all until, with our birth, we find ourselves imbedded in physical life. It becomes our journey to experience this life. Before all things and times were equally present to our awareness, but in our current physical existence one moment follows the next and there is a kaleidoscope of things of which we can be aware. Because of this we need a tool to define that experience for us. We created the ego, like a lens, that we hold between us and our world of experience. The ego, our tool, begins to make the judgments that define our physical world. It describes what is out there, what is possible, and what is not, within this sphere of experience. It assigns value to these judgments to cement them in our awareness. This is fine for a while. It is as we intended. We are busy experiencing and that is our goal. In fact, this would be fine forever except that we notice that within our experience things are not so simple. Through awareness to coincidence we see that the meanings our ego has assigned don't always fit. We look closer, but when we do, because we are holding our tool of the ego in front of us, looking closer doesn't produce a clearer view. Instead the thing we are looking for disappears altogether. This is fine. We go on experiencing, but we are nagged by that coincidence with a meaning seemingly just at the periphery of our awareness.

Eventually by trying different techniques we find that if we drop the lens of the ego, the coincidence blossoms instead of disappearing. It feels so different that we grab the ego again, as is our habit, to try to figure it out. Our ego jumps in and judges the situation unworthy of attention in order to convince us to return to its brand of experience. This is what happens when we attempt envisioning from a level of the mind body balance alone. We forget clarity for a while again. And so it goes, until we sense that the purpose of our being is no longer to simply experience. It is to experience from the viewpoint of pure clarity. Through the fractured and momentary connections we have had we have now come to know that there is more and we want it. We hunger for the connection to power beyond *and* for physical experience. Normal life, as we have known it, is no longer enough. Left solely to the ego's device, our life is no longer bringing us what we desire. It has become unmanageable by the ego alone.

I first accepted surrender sufficient to begin my experience of clarity as a result of the teachings of Tom Brown Jr. Within the culture of the Apache, clarity, and the pure connection to power beyond is called "inner-vision" or the "voice of spirit within." Among the Apache, inner-vision is considered the source of all true awareness. In the language of conscious envisioning this combination of surrender, clarity and purity is the first consciously functioning harmonic. When these three notes ring through our awareness the new harmonic tone created is inner-vision. To walk in harmonic perception, where spirit is the foundation of every moment, where spirit defines the meaning of every shadow, where spirit speaks in every sound, is to experience the harmonic of inner-vision.

Like many of my early experiences my first experience of inner-vision was seemingly trivial and innocuous. At the time I did not imagine the reverberations it would cause all through my life. The lesson had as its purpose the acceptance of the Earth as my teacher. Accepting Mother Earth as teacher is both easier and more difficult than it sounds. To relax our vigilance, our self-direction, and allow someone else to lead is a release, but when that teacher asks something outside our comfort zone, something silly or something impossible, the release turns to a dare.

Early in my relationship with the Earth I was sent out to look for a lesson. I wandered into the woods having some faith that there would be a lesson, but I had no idea of what the specific lesson would actually be. I wandered, unable to let my mind slow down, unable to relax. I followed my curiosity. From one tree, to a glade, further, I wandered until frustration began to erupt. I reasoned that since I was wearing my tennis shoes and was not really in contact with the Earth that perhaps I could not hear the lesson. Perhaps Earth Mother was waiting for me to do all I could to be worthy of her lesson. So I slipped off my shoes in mid-stride and walked on.

The area I was in was forested in medium-sized pines and scrub oak. The oak came to the level of my chest and the pines were branched over my head so I had a clear view through the forest but I could not readily see the ground around me. I caught sight of a particularly white tree trunk. It was dead and sun bleached. I went toward it thinking surely the lesson would come from that tree, some track on its bleached surface that I had never seen before or some other mystery. The scrub oak blocked my way and I was forced to circle around before I could reach the tree.

Near it I stood silent for a while and tried again to quiet myself. Then I inspected the trunk of the tree. I gazed at what was left of the branches above. Frustrated, I finally gave up, "she cannot always be waiting to teach me," I thought. At that moment an idea popped into my head. It was not a voice really but had the same quality. "Hey stupid, go find your shoes!" My first reaction was, "What! Who cares about my old tennis shoes?" "Just go find them," the idea returned, and when I turned to retrace my steps, the 'voice' said, "Never take the same trail twice or you'll never learn anything." This was something Stalking Wolf had told Tom Brown. Stalking Wolf avoided going and returning by the same route all his life.

I have a fairly good sense of direction, and I could see through the woods fairly well, at least above the scrub oak, so I didn't think I'd have too much trouble. I thought I'd just finish the rough half circle I'd started by being detoured around the clump of scrub oak on my way to the dead tree in the first place. At the very least I thought I'd be able to see my tracks when I crossed my trail.

After ten minutes or so I had to admit that I had missed my trail. I hadn't seen any tracks. None of the scrub looked familiar. At that point I couldn't even see the white trunk anymore! The day was cloudy, and I had only a vague notion of the direction of camp. At this point another idea popped into my awareness. "Use *inner-vision*. Ask with the language of the heart." Each of us, through spirit, is connected to everything else, yet through the common language of logic and words we cannot access this information. Only through using inner-vision and speaking in the language of the heart can we tap into this vast resource. I had practiced inner-vision before, but only in a setting where I had nothing at risk. As the thought of using inner-vision coursed through my brain, another thought, which seems quite irrational now but which at the time grew large and powerful, followed. I became afraid of going back without my shoes. Somehow, though it was warm and I had a back up pair of footwear, I became convinced that others would know I had lost my shoes, and I would feel ridiculed.

This somehow got me over a hump to where I was willing to try to locate my shoes by inner-vision alone. I had learned a very simple procedure. I simply faced a direction and asked myself. "Is this the right way?" Immediately after asking I paid attention to how my body felt. The idea is that spirit is always trying to get through to us using whatever means available. This is because it is the way it is. "I am that I am." "Spirit is that it is." The feeling in the first direction was a loud "NO," so I turned a few degrees. In a direction I would not have guessed, my body's response was one of excitement; in other directions, it was dejection. But I did not stop there. Next, I asked how far and in my mind I marked out a short distance. "No." a little further? "NO." Further? "Yes." Further yet? "No stupid, I told you they are back there!" Sometimes my inner-vision can get a little peeved at me.

I couldn't walk directly to the spot my inner-vision had picked out, but I kept my eyes glued to it as I made my way. As I got closer I began to recognize the patterns of the bush, and sure enough there were my shoes! When I saw them a chill went through my body and in my mind I reviewed the events of the last few minutes. I had had truly no idea where my shoes were. I had had no idea and yet I had walked unerringly to them. I reviewed the sensation I had felt when I found the right direction and distance, because it was different from what Tom Brown had described when he was teaching the technique. In that moment as I bent over to pick up my shoes, I realized that my world had changed forever. I could no longer feel that I could be lost or that I could lose something that is important to me. The lesson penetrated far beyond the act of finding the shoes or any other object. I knew that difficulty was not a matter of possibility or impossibility just of clarity, of willingness, and of surrender.

There is a sense within all of us that allows us to know that which should logically be beyond our grasp. There is nothing mysterious about this feeling of inner-vision. We all use it all the time. We say, "it just doesn't feel right", or, "something is making me uneasy." This is the same sense. It is our subconscious trying to get through to our conscious. The next time this happens to you spend some time with it. Rather than pursuing the object of your inner-vision logically, feel the sense of inner-vision itself and recognize what is happening. Your inner-vision is trying to tell you something. In contemplating the feeling in its pure state you are much more likely to get the information. Each time your inner-vision tries to speak up over the clamor of your logical mind it does so for a reason. There is the given instance, the thing you have forgotten, but there is also much more. There is the possibility that you will recognize its voice. With that recognition vistas open that have led the sages of all times.

Purity in your relationship with power beyond means that you hold that relationship first. Ultimately that relationship is all there is. Inner-vision is the voice of that relationship. All other things of which the ego is so fond are symbols of that relationship. It is hard to imagine the world in this way. That every tree, every storm, every car, encounter, fear and love, is a symbol of your relationship with your version of power beyond.

Even as I write it my ego guides me to use the words *nothing more than a symbol* ... as if a *thing* being a symbol of power beyond is somehow lessening it. This is the work of the cloudy lens. In reality every tree, every storm, every raised voice, hurt, and joy, is a symbol of our individual connection to the Great Mystery, to all power, to the most fantastic version of ourselves and the world imaginable. Awareness of this connection is to raise the world in majesty and wonder almost beyond our comprehension.

God And Evolution

With the formation of the first harmonic we are half way up the pyramid. This is a place where a secondary resistance can build. We are starting to see that readiness entails a lot more than being calm or being interested. It is easier, more traditional, and in many ways more comfortable, not to think that man is involved in the creation of what we see, feel, and think of as real, even as a partner. It is more comfortable to think that the greenness of the trees is either "God" creating it alone or that "evolution" is the path that led to green trees, without the involvement of any consciousness at all. I have stayed away from these words so as not to invoke this argument until now. Neither of these lines of thought, though we have fought over them throughout history, seems to matter anymore. On our journey toward conscious envisioning we are simply looking for the place in ourselves where we observe the world purely. God and evolution are both points of view relative to power beyond and as such, these defined points of view obscure the process of envisioning. Dr. David Hawkins, in his book "Power vs. Force," describes these points of view as "Positions." He notes that progress along a line of spiritual development brings us to a place where all "positions" must be put aside. Without this, he says, true awareness cannot enter.

As long as we assume a position, or point of view, our awareness is filtered by that position and it becomes a precondition determining what can be seen or known.

Your understanding will always depend on the point of view you take in the beginning. If two people take different positions they may end up in a fight. In my language, when two individuals envision completely differently, they will not even know of each other, but if they envision everything except a few details together they will feel their conflict very consciously and acutely. Conflict comes, not from holding widely different positions, but from holding very similar, but non-identical, positions very firmly. This firmness or stubbornness of position is natural when the process is unconscious. But, if we become conscious of our envisioning we will be able to see that we have merely taken up a position. Instead of fighting we could laugh at ourselves. In consciousness we can find relief in knowing that we don't have to hold our troublesome position any longer, nor do we have to accept the position of another. Further, we may feel grateful for the conflict that brought our unconsciously held position to light. In consciousness of it we can choose to release it and bring ourselves that much closer to purity.

Personally, with my art, I am looking for the greatest possible freedom to live and to experience. For me it isn't helpful to try to adopt the beliefs of others especially concerning what power beyond is. My experience is richest when I allow that power to simply be with me in each moment without even my own tendency to name it. Then the world is filled with energy, and love, and all possibilities.

Attention to coincidence is the symbol of readiness. Your consciousness is awakening to the fact that reality is not what you thought it was. You are coming to see that reality is the method power beyond is using to communicate with you. Because there is only one true relationship, there can be no compromises on our path toward conscious envisioning. Any compromise is the creation of a contingency upon your version of power beyond. Essentially it is an attempt to assert control over that which is beyond our control.

The essential questions are bubbling to the surface. Are you ready to admit that the current situation is unmanageable by you? Are you willing to accept that a power beyond yourself may be able to do better? Are you willing to surrender the control of your ego, not to another individual, not to a guru, or a fanatic, but to your own current, personal understanding of power beyond?

Interlude: Why Bother?

We have taken this whole journey just to arrive at this point. Like looking back after climbing a steep trail, it is the vista seen when you have arrived that allows you to understand where you are and why you climbed the trail.

We are cultivating our experience of connection with power beyond. This is the source of the magic in conscious envisioning. We are looking for the experience of knowing that our relationship to power beyond is in the primary position. This means that we experience ourselves, then power beyond, and then the world. We are looking to have an ongoing conscious awareness of this relationship. In this way we can know, through experience, the partnership role our awareness plays in creating our experience. This is the process of awakening into conscious envisioning.

In doing this we are looking for the clarity that will allow us to see the world around us as it actually is in each moment. We have accepted that the world as we have seen it is not real. It is an illusion. Clarity is the gift of knowing the true relationship between power beyond, the world, and us. Knowing this will release us from the habitual vision that has built up through the course of our lives. This surrender of our habitual vision must be voluntarily. No one can coerce this surrender or it will simply become acceptance, or abdication, or cooperation plus resentment and the resulting awareness will simply be another layer of the illusion. This is why this is the hardest step and the one most difficult to understand.

To come to this willingness we must understand that our adherence to habitual vision is a behavior that is *repetitive* and *detrimental* to our growth, and that to believe our awareness or experience to change while doing the same thing over and over is an *unmanageable* belief, by ordinary means. We must accept that we are in denial of the process that traps us and though it feels hard because the quality of the illusion is very high, it is created by our very illusion itself. If we can accept this circular situation is active in our experience we can create the possibility of our awakening.

We still feel that, at times, our circumstances aren't so bad and that if we tried hard enough we would be able to control our lives. In this belief we have maintained our position of avoiding the need to surrender completely. But now, having experienced surrender at least to some extent, we can acknowledge that we have begun a journey. Even though we may still, occasionally, have trouble recognizing the consequences of holding onto our insanity, having come this far, our eventual awakening is no longer in question. The relative comfort of the collectively-envisioned reality will never be quite as comfortable again. Once our eyes and hearts have opened to clarity and we have felt our pure relationship to power beyond something essential has changed. As previously mentioned, relapses can be extreme, but our awakening has begun.

> I was talking to a man who told me he didn't have a problem with stress because he exercises. It is remarkable to me how sold we can become on one point of view. Until a few 'experts' convinced doctors to start telling people that exercise was good for stress it wasn't very popular. There are bygone eras when

exercise was thought to be unhealthy, now it is thought to be 'the cure' for stress.

Consider this, our genetic makeup has been evolving not for thousands of years, or tens of thousands, but for hundreds of millions of years.[29] During the last thousand years our genetics haven't really changed at all. We are basically the same animal we were when we were living off the land. For the very early millions of years it is reasonable to assume that we were not as communal as we are now. For almost all of this early time human beings were both prey and predator. Our current huge system of societal development is a very high order of development. There were many steps along the way while we, very gradually, developed our current social ability. There was also a long time when we were on our own. On the individual and on the communal level systems were evolved to handle both situations, since we were both predator and being prey. Our stress response is basically the response, on the individual level, to being preyed upon. It follows that one of our basic responses to stress was designed to be able to run from saber-toothed tigers. We ran first as individuals and then as groups.

As an individual, when running from a saber-toothed tiger, it is reasonable to sacrifice everything in order to get away. It really doesn't matter if you sprain your knee and develop arthritis later, or even if you soon get pneumonia. All that matters is making sure that

---

[29] The beginning of civilization via organized farming in Mesopotamia began six thousand years ago. Perhaps less organized farming preceded this by ten thousand years. It is still insignificant relative to evolutionary time scales.

the tiger doesn't eat you. Running was a very appropriate response to saber toothed tiger attack; basically, exercise vigorously, for as long as it takes. The thing is, no human being ever actually outran a saber-toothed tiger or any other similar predator. We didn't evolve along the lines of the gazelle. Our top speed is significantly below that of any respectable pure hunter and, yet, we have come to dominate the Earth. It must be that we found other ways to handle this stress besides exercise. In fact, exercise was, and is, only a preliminary method of stress handling. It is useful in a crisis but ultimately not all that effective as a long-term answer. Anyone, or any group, who just kept running and running and did nothing else became tiger chow. We are the survivors because we found other mechanisms.

Instead of just running human, beings learned to cooperate. Like many animals we learned the value of the herd in assuring the survival of the group. It is true that a small number might be taken from time to time but the group would survive. And, since we were, and are, smarter than the average herd animal, we developed strategies to use high level cooperation methods to foil the attack of predators so that we would all have a chance to survive. I would imagine that some of us distracted the attackers while the less well equipped secured their hiding places. The more skillful might find defensible positions from which to face the attacker. We knew that although for us it was life or death, for the saber tooth it was just lunch. For the prey it is not required to kill in order to survive. We simply had to convince the attacker that there was another lunch less troublesome than this one.

Imagine what it would be like for you if you were not the one carrying a spear or if you weren't the best fighter, or if it simply wasn't your turn. What you would do is run like heck, then duck, hide and become very, very quiet. Rabbits use this strategy. They bound, bound, bound in a zigzag designed to confuse the eye as to which way they are going next, and then they hide. They even have a white tail to catch your eye producing a focus, and then they tuck it under and become very still. Often they are right there hiding behind something very small like a twig or a slightly higher clump of grass. But, because they had been so prominent in your vision, with their tail and the fast motion, and because they suddenly became so still and quiet, they seem to have disappeared. In fact, for most of us who aren't rabbit hunters we may assume that the rabbit is gone, that somehow we just didn't see where it went. The rabbit sits quietly for a while and then slowly moves off.

Humans had this option, too. We ran, and then we stopped and dropped into silence, quieting even our breath. Some of us might distract the animal and confront it for a while to discourage it. This way more of us survived. Sometimes one of us didn't make it, and it was sad. We wandered back to our shelters and sat around the campfire telling our stories. We talked and laughed and cried. We mourned and our feelings were out in the open and then we lay down to sleep knowing that we had come into balance again. There is a lot more to handling stress than exercise.

This is also born out by medical studies showing that the longevity of the benefit of exercise in stress related disease is very short. As soon as you stop running, if that is all you do, the benefit is gone (in two weeks according to the studies) and then the tiger eats you. These days that means that your risks for strokes and heart attacks goes right back to pre-exercise levels. Whereas, for even the most basic mind body training program, the benefit lasts as long as anyone has cared to study it. Currently, there are studies for five years and a few for ten years. The benefit still persists. Ultimately, exercise is important for staying in shape, but as a stress reliever its benefit is dependent upon continuing it forever and ever with no lapses for injury, fatigue, vacations, or forgetting to pay your gym bill.

Conscious Envisioning is not a stress program *per se*, but it is dependent upon the ability to come into balance. A life dominated by the mind has brought us to the technological era and that has its good and its bad points. Observing our individual and communal response to technology from computing to saturation advertising, from automobiles to health care, I believe technology will be seen to have had a huge impact upon our evolutionary path. It may take the perspective of a few million years to look back and see this, but as for the main thrust of our evolutionary journey, harmonic sensing has been with us all along.[30] It is possible that our continued survival will depend upon our bringing into balance the truth of harmonic sensing with what technology has given us. Ultimately, bringing harmonic

---

[30] I cannot prove this to you. I have come to believe it through the study of primitive survival skills and awareness, including animal tracking. Harmonic awareness is found in all primitive cultures and simply is essential to survival in nature.

awareness to consciousness in envisioning may be the only way that we can withstand the stressful effects of technology itself.

Does this discussion seem like an aside? It isn't really, because, the step we are heading for on the pyramid is the letting go of expectations. There is one more step to prepare ourselves and then we must really let go. Currently, one of our largest, unconscious, expectations is that technology will save us. I doubt it. Just as with running from the saber-tooth tigers this illusion may seem, for a while, like a good idea. When the tiger is gaining on you, whether the tiger is the stress of technological society, your personal high blood pressure, your anger, or your pain, you will to have to let go of the illusion that something outside yourself is going to save you, or the results are going to hurt. I think many of us personally, and all of us collectively, may be beginning to feel that hurt. If we keep running, and keep maintaining the belif that the increasingly rapid development of new technologies will fix the damage of our old ones, our expectations may be disappointed. Is it all just a great big mistake? Not to me. It is an opportunity to come awake. What do we need to be ready?

Climbing To The Top

Rigorous Honesty

When you look back over your shoulder and in truth the tiger is gaining on you, what does it take for you to actually see and accept this truth? It requires rigorous honesty with yourself. If you lie to yourself and pretend you are outrunning the tiger, it just isn't going to turn out well in the end.

The path of our unconscious envisioning is demonstrated by the multiple definitions of many words. This allows us the option of choosing which one we want. Will we use the blaming option or the descriptive one? It depends on which lens, ego or power beyond, that we are holding to our eye.

rig·or·ous
1. harsh, strict, or difficult in nature
2. extremely precise and exacting
3. severe and extreme to experience
4. precise and formalized

Encarta® World English Dictionary

The definition of "rigorous" I have chosen to use in respect to "rigorous honesty" is the second or fourth but not the first or third. If you instinctively chose the first or third definitions ask yourself why. Does a vengeful god drive your choice? The relationship you choose in process towards conscious envisioning is built in the first three steps. Often, our society, or our egos, pretend that the step toward honesty is the first step on the path toward integrity or toward happiness but it just isn't so. In fact, taking the step toward honesty prematurely, without contact with power beyond, is to experience harshness and difficulty. Rigorous honesty, without clarity in connection to power beyond, is severe in judgment and extreme in severity because we do not know what is true or where truth comes from. The ego is left to decide in the vacuum of its own judgment. Separated from the source of real awareness we cannot actually know. We can only know what we have been told, accepted from authority, or what we think, which, left to our own devices, is always changing.

Rigorous honesty is about looking closely at what we say and do. Are we cutting the corners of what we have witnessed in order to make it more acceptable to those around us, or, in order to manipulate a certain outcome? Can we imagine a way of approaching rigorous honesty through a love of truth? If we can there is no need for difficulty or harshness. There is no reason for severity or extremity. There are many programs and methods of studying honesty in our lives. Twelve step programs detail a simple approach of looking at our past experiences in detail. Often people focus on the bad or reproachful aspects of their pasts but in the steps there is also a mandate to be honest about what we do well, what comes easily to us, and what gifts we have been given. Once the list is assembled it is suggested that it be shared with power beyond as it is understood and with another human being. This is important because it is the acting out of our efforts to become rigorous in our honesty. It is also important because this verbal sharing helps us to see that what is in our past that need not be judged. It simply is. What matters now is the level of honesty that we allow ourselves and what the results of that honesty can be.

Within rigorous honesty there can be a simple moving toward our goal of complete inward and outward expression of what we know to be our truth through the experience of clarity. This is like walking toward a light at the end of a tunnel. There may be many branches in the tunnel but only one has actual, pure, light streaming into it. Others are reflections or pale images created by our ego in its effort to maintain control. Various ego creations cannot be distinguished from one another because no particular ego creation is any truer than another.

As with the previous steps the option to reach for rigorous honesty is only available to us because of the prior step, in this case, the experience of purity. Without purity, honesty is not possible because our relationship with the origin is clouded or inconsistent. Purity is built upon the fleeting feelings of clarity that came in response to our surrender of value judgment. Each step is held in place by moving on, continuing to climb. It continues this way until we reach the top and the change of our being can be held in balance all at once.

If we do choose not to become honest, one simple act or thought of dishonesty will break the purity of our connection. Without that purity of connection we will deny what we have known through clarity; in the next moment we will take back the right to value judge and we will return to our ordinary lives. Struggle will come to us again where magic once was. In comparison to purely perceived clarity, where there is no question, no difficulty, no harshness or level of strictness, we will again experience uncertainty, doubt, and fear. Although we may need to be reminded from time to time as we come and go from our willingness surrender, each time it is more clear, more enlivening. It is possible that the very reason for our taking up the reins of the ego again is just so we can once more enjoy the recognition of clarity, so that we can re-taste the discovery of purity. We may be like lovers who like to pick fights just to make up.

We cannot actually change our worthiness because that is a product of our connection to power beyond, but we can choose how we will demonstrate it to ourselves. We do not control being connected just whether we are aware of that connection. Similarly, we do not choose to envision, we only choose whether to be conscious of it. Perhaps the experience of purity is too poignant for us in this moment. Perhaps it is too much to surrender and we still cling to ego-oriented ideas of our needs. If so, we are also completely capable of envisioning ourselves as inadequate. In the absoluteness of our actual reality we can envision anything, including the illusion of our worthlessness. Amazingly, we can even choose to envision our lack of worthiness through connection to power beyond, consciously! We may envision that we must become pure in order to be worthy of connection. Any simple self-deception will work and will feel true in the power of our unconscious envisioning. But, if you look closely enough at these self deceptions you will find that they are based on some sort of value judgment and are sponsored by some idea of a vengeful power.

For instance:

I am hungry.

I am tired.

I need more money.

I need a better job.

If only my lover would ... (add anything here).

If only my parents hadn't ...

I wouldn't be so ....

If only....

All of these are value judgments about the condition of our being. I *feel* hungry is a description of an experience. Notice that a descriptive statement is inherently more honest than a statement of being. You are a human being. You may feel hungry. You may be a human being who feels hungry but your feeling of hunger has no basis in who you are. Feeling hungry, you may choose to eat or not depending upon the clarity inherent in the next moment. Often, attention to clarity will transmute the feeling of hunger into another feeling, and another, that will lead you to know yourself and your own experience more fully and more deeply. Within that experience you will have found what you were hungry for, possibly not food at all, and your experience will have changed.

I guarantee that if the saber-toothed tiger jumps out at you, you will forget all about your feelings of hunger and you will become a human being feeling the fear of being eaten. Your essential being will not have changed but the feelings you are having will have changed significantly. Afterwards, perhaps, there will be time to nourish your physical self or wash your wounds or be close to your loved ones, but within clarity you will perceive exactly what your body desires. In supplying that need your experience becomes one of fulfillment. If we block this experience with the simple, seemingly trivial, difference between the words "I am" and "I feel," we label our being rather than describing an experience. We will be telling ourselves a lie and with this lie our connection to power beyond fractures. Our thoughts will again be only of the ego and our experience will again become ordinary. It is possible that even in labeling our self *as* hungry, we will so constrain our feelings into the ego's realm that we will not feel the saber-tooth's eyes as it watches from its hiding place. We will be one fatal step late starting our run.

When we fall from wherever we have climbed on the pyramid we do not simply fall to the step before. We always fall completely. Just as the addict who picks up after many years of recovery and find that the disease of addiction has been waiting all along, we experience our denial as strong as it ever was, perhaps even stronger. And, once we are within the illusion again, all the same attributes that were present in the beginning exert their influence again. The comfort of the herd is indeed comfortable. The fact that your are heading in a direction you may not want to go is obscured, at least for a while, by being again in the middle of the collective experience.

Instead of finding ourselves falling we also have the option of continuing on. Each step is secured by the next step, which enables the next, until the full harmonic is built. When the entire pyramid is climbed and each step embraced, when the whole harmonic rings out into the universe of your personal being, it will have its own balance and life. At that point it will take an event of significance to rock or destroy your recovery. At that point you will have to choose with knowledge to succumb again. It will not be falling from a precarious position, but jumping from a secure location.[31]

Releasing Expectations

Armed with rigorous honesty and with the experience of allowing our lies to be out in the open, we will become aware of the next step. It is the releasing of all the energy and effort we have been placing at the service of our guilt, our fears and our resentments. Through rigorous honesty we will be able to see that these are not facts of existence. They are merely positions we have taken to support the lies we have told ourselves and others. Coming into this knowledge we will have a choice. As at each previous step, our ego will present this choice so fast that if we are not paying attention we will miss that we even had a choice. We will simply feel overwhelmed and unconsciously choose to return to our old ways. But, if we have sincerely turned over value judging, if we have savored clarity and cherished our pure relationship with power beyond, if we have begun to enjoy being rigorously honest, then there will be a moment when we will see that our guilt, fear and

---

[31] The steps I describe can be related to the steps of a 12-step program. The step in this book of becoming honest and the next step of releasing resentments I use as a combination of the middle steps 4 through 9. Willingness to work these steps often separates those who succeed in substance recovery from those who relapse. A structure such as AA uses may be required. At this point I see the focus on the essence of the steps: Honesty and Willingness.

resentment are not based on an *actual* reality but on what we *expect* of reality.

With this realization we have envisioned the choice to release these expectations. Rather than expect our loved ones to behave in certain ways we can simply choose to love them and observe what they do. Rather than fear the way our body may feel or appear to our judgment we may simply feel it honestly and listen to its needs. Rather than blame others for our situation we can simply know ourselves and know our relationship with power beyond. Rather than decide what others are expecting of us and trying to anticipate their desires we can choose to simply be ourselves and trust that this will be best. We can choose to feel ourselves in concert with creation and move from one moment to another in harmony with all that surrounds us. Rather than running from our next lesson, we can choose to embrace it fully and squeeze every bit of life from it. Will health follow this rebalancing? My instinct is that even our definition of health is in need of a rigorously honest reappraisal. Possibly "true" health does *follow* rebalancing. Perhaps true health is *created by* rebalancing. [32]

Shame And Denial, Purposeful Presence

After the release of expectations and the resulting release from guilt, fear and resentment, the final step is into the full blossoming of the harmonic. It is as simple as accepting all the preceding steps simultaneously. Again, and always, we have choice. At these moments we will feel that choice acutely. In wakefulness we will feel our choice and know the results of our

---

[32] People often argue over the definition of the word "true." In this case I mean a reproducible experience among many different individuals.

choice as our own. This pathway takes courage. I takes courage to know that the power we have is immense and to step into that power with clarity and with our true self revealed and in partnership with our personal concept of power beyond. To do this with humility and to remain in that power without value judging our self or the world around us is the essence of this change. To remain in the purity of our connection without forming expectations will ensure the formation of the next step, which is the release from shame and denial. This is not a step like the others preceding it. There is nothing to do. It is simply a realization. It is the realization that there is no longer anything to be in denial of and that shame no longer exists in you. The result is a presence that comes into you and begins to radiate from you.

Shame and denial cannot be released by simple measures. There are other pathways, other traditions, to attain the attributes I have discussed but I don't know of any shortcuts. Imagine a mountain climber who has been laboring for hours in thin air. He has been in a state of constant effort requiring everything of him. He has had to strip himself bare to make his journey. Every hint of resistance, of holding back, has been sacrificed to reach the top. Now he is finally nearing the summit, but in his effort he is almost unaware. Then, there is the last step to the top of the mountain and he slowly comes to see that there are no more steps to take. The realization washes over him that the summit has been reached. Looking around himself he sees that the entire world lies below. He remembers all that he has done, and given up to come here. All shame has dropped away because there is nothing left. All the notions of mundane life he began his climb with have been left along the way. There is nothing left to deny because there is nothing left hidden. The effort, for now, is finished.

Now, there is a new-ness born in him. He is standing, circling, holding and cherishing his prize. All his effort has brought him this precious view. Recovering his breath the choice comes to him again. It is no longer framed in thoughts of quitting. There are no more worries of failure or feelings of inadequacy. His goal has been reached, but even so he could still allow his ego to claim the prize. He can accept the thoughts of better, than worse than. It would be so easy from this height! Or he can remain in his pure experience establishing a simple presence. Always, we have this same choice. It is our nature, our gift, and yet always our risk. To choose to stay in the pure experience while holding in balance all the measures taken to arrive is the capstone of the Pyramid. To turn this moment of presence into your normal way of being is to solidify all that has gone before. It is to carry this presence with you into the world. It is to assume your new posture of *purposeful presence* in the world. It is to say who you are and why you are here. It is a statement that cannot be made in words. It is pure experience.

The Posture of Recovery, And Gratitude

I call this section the "posture of recovery" because it is the healing from all positions and addictions of body and mind. It is the release into spirit that results from surrender and induces the feeling of gratitude. From here envisioning is not colored by the past, by unknown needs or agendas. Envisioning flows through the posture of recovery with the pure intent of power beyond unaffected by the ego. The posture of recovery is characterized by the persistent feeling of gratitude and it is an awareness that is not new to us. We are in recovery of this feeling, this attitude. It is a balance and an awareness that is our natural state.

The ego can now assume its intended role. It describes the world; it is an interface, a tool of spirit. The posture of recovery is the end of the long journey of development of the ego into its final form. It is the taking up of control and then the voluntary surrendering of it.

Human beings have always sought knowledge of the basis of worldly reality. We have always sought to understand the mechanism of its creation. In recent times our discoveries have brought us to research that is both scientific and spiritual. Our greatest physicists have become spiritualists. The Apache also studied the world and came to the same place in understanding. The discovery that we must acknowledge is that we are *inside* the system we are studying. Our scientific goal expects us to remain outside the system we are investigating. It is believed that this will give results independent of us as the observers, but in the system of reality the separation of observed and observer is illusion. Actual reality cannot be experienced until the illusion is dissolved.

We also know that the world and everything within it is composed of energy. Particles are not different substances but rather very tightly packed locations of energy. All the different forms of large particles become more similar as we look more closely. All forms of energy consist of the same ultimate energy. This energy is thought of in many different ways depending upon the observer's state of being, but individuals who have climbed the ladder of awareness come to agree that the most basic energy comes from somewhere beyond what we know and see as ordinary. When the observer has walked the road of expanding awareness up to the transition where awareness of spirit becomes real, the basic form of energy is seen as energy of love. Here, love is not an emotion; it is the energy of essential being.

You perhaps thought I was going to say electromagnetic energy is the basic energy. While this may be most commonly believed it is not so. Even the brain creates electromagnetic energy right? *Avant-guard* scientists use electromagnetic sensors to detect ghosts and psychic energy. Why is love primary energy? Here is how I understand it. Electromagnetic energy is an outgrowth of being. Love is the energy of intent. In a way I think of electromagnetic energy as a by-product of the energy of love as it is in the act of creation. It is like a car engine that creates heat as a by-product of creating motion. Ultimately, for our purpose here, it doesn't matter what name you use to describe the energy of formation if we can agree that the world is composed of a basic form of energy.

As the energy that forms the world flows from power beyond, through us and into the world, it comes through the lens of our personal relationship with the world. We are, in essence, the interface on a personal level. What matters is our personal version of power beyond and our personal relationship with the world. This is our most basic level of being. It is the level at which envisioning functions. The intention present in this interface is not carried by power beyond as a "desire" as we might humanly desire something; rather it is an inherent part of the structure of creation. It may or may not become manifest at this time dependent on our action of being at the center of the interface. In order to come to the fullness of ourselves in creation we must come to authenticity in this interface. This includes much more than our speech and actions. We carry our current level of authenticity through the *posture* we take in our lives.

The word "posture" means something to all of us. Usually, our parents told us to stand up straight so that our posture looked good to them and others. The military teaches the posture of attention as a way of conveying both obedience and respect. Each modern generation has adopted its own physical posture, slumping this way or that to differentiate it from the generations before. Non-verbal communication is said to contain ninety percent of the information we communicate. This non-verbal communication is posture in dynamic motion. I think of posture as relating to the most basic expression of being, that is we carry and demonstrate our relationship through our posture. We are in a certain posture relative to everything that exists. Our basic posture affects the flavor of awareness that we bring to every interaction. The firmness with which we hold our posture reflects our level of resistance to change. We are individuals; none of us can hold exactly the same posture and our differences are a reflection of our uniqueness.

Just as we may choose to look at the world through the lens of the ego or the lens of power beyond, power beyond looks into the world through the lens of our personal posture. Though we did not and do not create the world, we are involved in its creation through our most basic relationship expressed by our posture. Our level of awareness is the key to our posture. If we choose to hold resentments, that will change the way everything comes into our awareness and this will affect our posture both physically and spiritually. If we choose to make value judgments this will be reflected in our posture and it will affect any kind of energy power beyond can express through us.

It does not serve us to curse or blame power beyond for the suffering in the world. The suffering of individuals and the collective is a result of the lens through which these events are both viewed and created. The energy of manifestation is freely given. The original intent of energy is the intent of love. It is our choice to allow that energy to be distorted by the lens of our ego or to put aside our limited versions of ourselves, allowing instead to be led by power beyond through the lessons of climbing the pyramid. Here the tool of gratitude returns to the forefront. A grateful attitude will defeat the ego's claim. It will defeat also the ego's blame. No matter what you see around you, it is not yours to judge. The experience of the world is just that; experience. In a 'Course In Miracles,' and in 'Conversations With God,' and in 'The Lives and Teachings of the Masters of the Far East,' and in 'Power vs Force,' on and on, even Christ's words upon the cross, "Forgive them Father for they know not what they do," all through our history, our wisest, our or most spiritual leaders teach us that all experience is acceptable. The richness of experience on the physical plane, no matter what that experience is, no matter how the ego cries out for it or against it, all of the stuff of life is expressed in the loving energy of creation. And, when we perceive it through the lens of power beyond we can be grateful for it.

A posture takes no specific point of view. A posture is not a *position*. A posture describes a method of being or the pure experience of being. In the language of envisioning it is our posture, both collective and individual, that holds any and all creations within the sphere of space and time.[33] The climbing of the pyramid is one process for experiencing consciously the posture we are holding. At each point we are given the choice of standing within our greatest self or within a limited view. At each point we may choose to control outcomes through the action of our ego or to surrender to the magic of what might be. It is the surrender of all positions that enables the posture of recovery. The posture of recovery is born directly from the authentic experience of self in each of us as we become willing to do *whatever it takes* to be our true selves. It is a state of being that comes into experience by the creation of harmonic awareness through a process such as climbing the pyramid. When we reach out to power beyond, when we allow ourselves to be pulled across the chiasm into clarity, gratitude is the human result of the transmission of loving energy flowing through into creation. The posture of recovery is held in time and space through recognition of gratitude.

What rings out when the harmonic is struck? What is it that you experience? Posture is an internal reflection. What is the outer reflection? It is "purposeful presence." This is what makes your individual posture visible among all others. This is the essential piece of expression that you bring into the outer world. This is what you are grateful to give to the world and it is with this act of giving that you are held in the harmonic of your posture of recovery, in your pure partnership with power beyond.

The art of conscious envisioning is what is possible when we become consciously aware of our posture and the harmonic we are singing to the world. It is not dissimilar to a

---

[33] I am describing the individual interface with the world and with power beyond. This is the seat of individual envisioning. The collective can also be seen as an individual, as a football team can be seen as a unified entity. It is for another time to develop the techniques for forming a group or collective into a unity for collective envisioning. At this point the unity in our human collective remains largely unconscious.

love affair where, at the beginning, only one person knows that they are in love. In this beginning this is, and always has been, power beyond. There has never been a moment when that love was in doubt because it is the very act of creation. And yet, we are just now systematically coming into our own consciousness of that love and creation. Throughout history the giants among us have held this awareness and the effects of their consciousness have passed down through the ages raising our over all collective consciousness. Now, it is time for many more of us to awaken.

When both sides of a human love affair are awake to their love and when the love is shared equally and consciously it is as if a miracle has happened. We spend our lives searching for and hopefully coming to live within such a relationship. Now, that pursuit may expand to include our relationship with the world as a whole through our relationship with power beyond. It is as simple as the choice we have been discussing all along. We stand in the flow of love creating the world. We may choose to look downstream and allow our ego to make value judgments about that creation. We know the experience that comes from that. Or, we may turn completely around and view the stream of creative love facing first, upstream, standing in our faith of the world behind us without even the need to look. I have said before that health is completely different from the absence of disease. It is just the same at any level of being. If we choose to look for disease, eventually we will find it. If we are immersed in health our experience will be simply what is intended.

Conscious envisioning flows from the posture of recovery. This is the note of our true-selves ringing into the world, and this is the fulfillment of our relationship to power beyond. In this way we may feel the love of our creator through each interaction we have. We will find ourselves willing to do our part without effort. And, with that, the world will give back to us all that we desire. This will be, not in trade, but because that is the way it works when we are in love.

To plan our envisioning with specificity through the use of our minds, our imagination and our conscious connection is a step that creates experience reliably only when it is done from a completely solid balance within the posture of recovery. To envision by design becomes much less needed when the posture of recovery is attained. Your inner desires and needs are not unknown to power beyond; rather they are part of your identity and thus they manifest without effort. Yet there still is a yearning to envision consciously and specifically, to steer the path of out lives or to consciously add to the lives of others. Within this yearning is the great temptation of the ego. To consciously use the mechanisms of the mind, and engage the ego without grasping control is the *Art*.

Simply maintaining a solid posture of recovery is miracle enough, but can you feel the disappointment of your ego in that statement? Doesn't it want to plan and create on its own? Practice pure posture until that urge fades and any need to plan comes unbidden by you, as if it comes from the very air around you. Then, your posture will be strong. Your mind, your imagination and your ego will be known for the simple tools they are. Your posture is your identity expressing the love of creation into physical form. Hold back the urge of the ego until it is nothing to your posture. Then will be the time.

Summary:

We have now discussed the last three steps up the pyramid and what is to be found at the top. We know that these steps are possible by only building the foundation harmonic. Then, even while experiencing that harmonic, we come to feel that there is more. As we look for what that might be, we come to see that we are still hiding from ourselves in many small ways. We are telling lies to ourselves and to others.

We knew that in telling those lies, we protect unconscious layers of denial. We are not yet in our purest relationship to power beyond. With this realization, most of us, perhaps all of us, lose our foundation harmonic again for a period of time. In recognizing our impurity we judge ourselves and return the ego to the forefront of our minds. We fall into ordinary life again. Still, despite our fall, we cannot forget where we have been. The flavor of the experience of being in pure relationship remains even though the details are, once more, hidden. This memory stimulates us to rediscover the first step.

The second, or third, or fiftieth time up the pyramid to the first harmonic, we finally come to the realization that even though we are telling lies, we don't fall, our footing has become firm enough to maintain, and we come to know, through clarity, and through our pure relationship to power beyond, that despite all, our relationship to power beyond is beyond any lie we can possibly tell. It is beyond any misdeed that we might do or hide. It is, in fact, beyond all simply human experience because it is an experience elevated by power beyond into its own realm.

With this understanding we can now undertake the next part of our journey. We can do the work in the relationship to power beyond that is ours to do. Not because we aren't worthy exactly as we are, but just because we can, and we desire to. With this we come to discover rigorous honesty and we use it to uncover our feelings of fear, guilt, and resentment. We came to see that it was not the details in the behavior of others that create our feelings; instead it is our own expectations that create the feelings.

Looking with rigorous honesty and remaining in clarity we see that this is nothing more than our ego again taking control. When we place our personal structure of expectation upon the world we usurp the power of creation, the power of magic. When we impose our expectations upon others or upon the world itself, we are essentially attempting to envision through the ego. The resulting resentments are nothing more than the ego's realization that this will never work. Fear and guilt are usually in place to camouflage and color this realization, but if we own our truth beyond fear and guilt we may decide to stop placing our energy into the world in this fashion. Thus we will come into an even greater clarity.

Through this increased clarity we will come to know intuitively when we are needed to speak or act. We will know intuitively what to say or do that will add naturally to the beauty around us. We will also understand when we can remain silent finding the beauty in what is already present. Residing in this honesty, free of fear and guilt, the purity of our relationship with power beyond will grow and clarity will become a constantly active level of awareness in our lives.

Soon we come to see that our previously constant companions of shame, guilt and denial to which we have devoted so much of our energy simply are no longer there. What had been so prevalent and so accepted that we felt would always be with us simply has become absent. Clarity and our relationship to power beyond crowds them out. Like the weight of a second skin they simply slide to the ground in some moment when we aren't looking. We realize then that we are finally free.

We look around ourselves as if we are freshly created. Without shame, denial, fear, or guilt: without our expectations we wonder who we really are. From within, through all the harmonics of our journey thus far, an answer appears. It is communicated not in words or in thoughts, but in a feeling, a knowing, a sense of becoming. Nothing true of ourselves can ever be expressed in simple words. Nothing of our great connection to power beyond can be reduced in any way. And yet, it rings out into the world through each of us. The energy each of us brings, combines into what happens and what does not happen, what is and what is not. Awakening to this truth and feeling it through our connection, our sense of being with and in power beyond, we know that this is our purpose and that we will fulfill it whether we are conscious of it or not. Our connection to power beyond does not depend upon our awareness of it just as our worthiness does not depend on who we think ourselves to be. We cannot sabotage the intention of power beyond. We can only imagine that our own will runs counter to it. Our illusion will not extinguish what is. Our lies, guilt, resentments and shame, our expectations, only serve to color our own experience in beauty or in judgment. It is only a question of *what* we desire to experience, that we will experience is not up to us.

When we realize the inevitability of this and simply rest in our pure relationship with power beyond, when we stop fighting for control, we can come to experience ourselves as suspended in aware-consciousness *between* the moments of creation. In this place, between one moment and the next, is where power beyond joins us from infinity and we are in partnership during the formation of the moment of now. This is where we exist in creative energy. This field between moments will become our next area of play and learning. All possibilities are contained between the moments of creation and from there we can, in partnership with power beyond, create something truly new. That there will inevitably be a next moment is the intent of power beyond and cannot be changed, but the warmth or chill of it, the smell and taste of it, the sound and color of it, how it will feel to us, these aspects are all up to us. Through our connection to power beyond we connect the world of possibility with the world of experience. We connect the world of loving creative energy that originates in power beyond with the material world of moments in space and time. Resting within the arms of power beyond we can see that the world is an illusion that we contain but which does not contain us, and in this knowing magic has become mechanism.

There is an energy flowing into the world that power beyond expresses as love. We can choose to look upstream into the flow of love by giving our attention first to power beyond and we will see all the beauty of infinite possibility. Or, we can look downstream by giving our attention first to the ego and see only the fixed results of creation. If we choose to look upstream, our ego, our self and individuality will not abandon us. There is no need for fear.

As we move into the next moment, the journey is reduced to one question and one choice. Once the pyramid is climbed we do not need to climb it again each day. Knowing that it is our conscious choice we can choose the harmonic of recovery in one positive step. Do we enter the next moment in a posture of addiction returning to a life of stubborn value judging, insisting upon our worthlessness, and consumed with a codependency that is fixated on the actions of others? Do we remain determined to hide our own lies through projection and denial until we are consumed by shame? Or, do we choose instead to come to rest in purposeful presence, thus holding our posture of recovery by entering the next moment in surrender of all value judgments to the clarity of a pure relationship with power beyond? Do we allow freedom in that relationship by choosing, in rigorous honesty, to release all expectations?

To live a life using the lens of power beyond, looking upstream into the energy of love flowing into the world, is to find the space between each moment. When we choose the posture of recovery we live consciously in the space suspended between moments observing and knowing naturally our place, time and actions. We will be immersed in joy through knowing the experience of love expressed into creation by power beyond. This is the relationship of conscious envisioning, neither in control nor controlled, in partnership with all of creation, seamlessly, timelessly, balanced in oneness.

The Art Of Conscious Envisioning

Chapter 4

Using Envisioning

Paying Attention to Coincidence

It will help as we go forward into actual techniques of envisioning to spend a moment going more deeply into the concept of coincidence. First, what is a coincidence exactly? Webster's definition of the word is:

1 exact correspondence, and

2 a seemingly planned sequence of accidentally occurring events.

Both of these definitions apply to our situation.

#1 Exact correspondence: Usually, as we become ready to awaken to awareness of envisioning, the element that attracts our attention is the feeling that "it," the coincidence, fits, too exactly to seem reasonably possible. There is a certain underlying element of approximation in what we normally expect from the physical world. The human mind is expert at balancing all this inexactness. Traffic moves close enough to what we expect for us to maneuver. People respond close enough to our expectations, usually, for us to carry on relationships. What actually jars us enough to notice is something that fits so exactly that it feels unnatural.

The type of coincidence that most often feels this way is the coincidence between a thought we have and something that then happens. This is the foreknowledge type of coincidence. For instance, you may know that the phone is going to ring and then it rings. This happens all the time. Or you may know that the phone is going to ring and it is going to be Bill and he is going to tell you that something specific happened. You may even know exactly how he is going to say it and for a minute you are living in rewind, or as if the program has been reset, *deja-vu*, like in the movie Matrix.

#2 A seemingly planned sequence of accidentally occurring events: This is the feeling that for things to have to worked out so well, that something or someone must be pulling the strings. For me this is the pull in the direction of recognizing the presence of a power beyond. This kind of coincidence becomes more and more common as the first envisioning of the flow develops to become a constant pursuit in life.

The coincidence that most commonly attracts our attention in the initial stage is a connection between a thought we have and an event that occurs. These can be complex multi-tiered events or simple connections. A purely physical level coincidence such as a ladder falling just as your cat is jumping so that she misses her jump and lands on your vase knocking it to the floor where it shatters is one thing. But, the foreknowledge that something is going to happen when you set the vase down there to answer your cell phone is much more interesting to me. Both are examples of coincidence but the first is evident on the physical level alone to anyone who might be observing. Only you know the second one in your thoughts just a moment before it happens.

What I hear from individuals in the beginning stages of noticing coincidence is the comment, "that was weird," or. "I was just thinking that." That is, there is recognition of the coincidence but it occurs in the past tense. One of the reasons why attention to coincidence is a heralding sign for the opening to envisioning is that as we pay more and more attention to coincidence, the gap between the actual coincidence and our recognition of it begins to decrease. Our consciousness of the coincidence becomes less and less in the past, but as long as our awareness continues to follow in time after the coinciding events there is no actual change in our lives. As we pay attention, and the temporal gap closes, there will come a day when we actually walk over to the phone waiting for the call that we know is going to come. Or through faith we will pick the vase back up and avoid whatever might have happened simply because of the feeling. At this point we have come to accurately identify the feeling of the impending coincidence and developed the instinct to react smoothly and efficiently to that knowledge. This is when things begin to change.

One of the coincidences that woke me up to this level of awareness occurred when I was learning to make fire with a hand drill. This is the method where you spin a small stick between the palms of your hands. It wasn't the actual fire making that taught me but the action of carving the end of the small stick. Often a Mullen stalk is used. Mullen is one of the stalky plants with a relatively soft center. This requires that when you are carving the end flat you have to hold the stalk right next to that end so that it doesn't split.

I carved one or two of these a week for several months in the process of gaining a beginning experience with the hand drill. I think that during the first ten attempts at carving I nicked the skin of my knuckle every time. Each time I had the feeling that I was going to cut myself right before I did it. The experience became so repetitive that after the tenth time I was getting tired of it and began to study it in earnest. I saw that the foreknowledge arrived on the knife stroke right before the one where I was going to cut myself. I had time to stop but I had to do it absolutely right then.

At that point a strange thing happened. I stopped cutting myself. Then, as soon as the stimulus was removed, I questioned the whole thing. It was as if I suddenly forgot the ten cuts that came before. Several of them weren't even healed yet. And then what happened? I promptly cut myself again which spawned a series of curses that went on much longer than required by the cut alone.

This occurrence, when we become sensitive enough to the feeling of foreknowledge to act upon it immediately, is a natural entrance to the flow. We simply begin to show up where we are needed, we coincidentally have what we need to have when we need to have it. At first we are surprised but soon it feels more natural. Events that used to take us by surprise, are not always anticipated, but are less surprising. We are thrown off balance less often. Sometimes, the people around us notice this change, but most often they do not. They are involved in their own lives as deeply as we are in ours.

This is one of the places where the lesson of humility, and the value of anonymity, can be felt first. When this attention to coincidence begins to manifest change in your life and if you begin to point it out to others, either for confirmation or for some level of taking credit, the awareness of coincidence may simply disappear altogether. What had been coming naturally will be a struggle again. In short, normal life will come to the surface of your experience again because the part of consciousness that needs validation and credit is the ego. The ego has no sensitivity, no actual awareness, of the level of life we are entering.

It is necessary, or at least human, for us to experience these ups and downs. It is part of the mechanism of surrender. It is the way we learn to keep our individual humanness and also move to a higher level of conscious awareness. Like many of the lessons on this path we continue to learn them our whole life. I have not yet reached a level where this isn't true.

Most recently this lesson reappeared in my life regarding an experience with road kill. It has always saddened me to see animals killed on the side of the road. I remember vividly driving with my father when I was about nine years old. It was the first time I made the connection between the dark stains on the road and blood. I didn't know it at the time but my father was also saddened and occasionally made ill by the amount of carnage sometimes littering our roads.

A few years ago I began an envisioning project regarding road kill. It seemed overwhelming to think about, or pray for, or help in anyway with the whole volume of the problem so I picked a one-mile section of road on my way to work. I didn't pick the worst place but it wasn't the best either.

I have heard people make comments like, "won't they ever learn," or "that deer just jumped out in front of me" but I think this displays a huge amount of anthropomorphism, lending human attributes to animals. Thinking about it and watching animals at the roadside I realized that to them it is more likely that roads are just hard places in the woods. I doubt they differentiate between them as particularly dangerous places or anything other than a place were there isn't much cover and nothing grows, although in Michigan they are also salty places and that can be good.

As human beings we know that if they would just wait for quiet they generally would be ok. But, to the animals this isn't really valid. To them they are at the one side of the road where there is all this noise; at night, there is glaring light that is blinding, and it gets worse and worse and the only thing to do is run. Sometimes that winds them up in the road getting splattered. For us, from the human perspective, we understand how dangerous roads are, but perhaps to an animal, the notion of a projectile coming along at fifty miles per hour just doesn't make sense.

So, I reasoned, this is an opportunity. Rather than try to explain it to the animals why they should stay out of the road I could simply leave some of my consciousness on my section of the road. I could simply envision that the animals along that section would consult me and I could then tell them if it was a good time to go, or a good time to wait. I have seen the instinctual way that animals move in the woods and I knew that going or waiting was something that would make sense.

For a year there were no kills on that section of road. Even the mile sections on either side saw improvements. It became easier for me to mourn the kills I saw on other sections because I felt I was doing what I could. But then, as usual, my ego found a way into my head. I began to wonder if I had just picked a place in the road where there weren't any kills. Perhaps, if I had more courage, I would have picked one of the worst places. The next day a deer died on "my section of road." It was exactly the next day. Looking at the kill I would bet that it happened only hours after I had traversed the section not thinking of lending my consciousness but rather of "maybe this is just a really safe section of road."

It was classic. From previous experiences I recognized the situation immediately. After all I had picked a section between a swamp and farm fields. There was a watercourse and cover. There had been kills there all the time the previous year and then none for a year. It didn't matter. I struggled with my envisioning for months while raccoons, opossum, and squirrels died there. At first I felt like they were dying on my watch, my section, like it was my responsibility. This didn't help at all. Gradually I had to re-climb the whole pyramid as it related to road kill and my section of road until I came to a place again where I could actually surrender and again envision in partnership with power beyond.

I have now been through this cycle twice. The first ego attack was launched through the belief in a 'safe section of road' and the second was more complicated. It sounds silly now but this is how my ego works. One day many months after my protracted recovery from the first ego attack I was envisioning down the road and there I chanced to see a red hawk eating a piece of its prey in a field along the road. The idea immediately appeared that perhaps in this section of road, somehow, the hawks and coyotes were really quick at removing the remains. Suddenly I knew what was happening. My envisioning was all fantasy and actually the hawks just right here were incredibly efficient.

In retrospect it is unbelievable. Red hawks don't even go in for carrion. It didn't matter. Once the ego finds a crack in the surrender, don't fight, just acknowledge it and start over. Re-climbing wasn't as hard this time. The idea was still hard to shake and I had to remember that time when I was nine. Even if the coyotes were picking up this particular road, I reasoned, they wouldn't stop to lick up the bloodstains. For a year there were no bloodstains. Not even my ego could deal with that.

PS. I have never told anyone where my mile is.

Upstream Energy

What would it be like to do an envisioning from the posture of recovery? Free from guilt and resentment, willing to allow denial to dissolve wherever it is found, in conscious contact with power beyond, knowing our worthiness? How would all these changes make envisioning different? Let's repeat our original envisioning of the flow but with this new perspective.

The steps are unchanged. I will indicate the new perspectives in [**bold**.]

The mind makes the decision to envision consciously. **[This is now the action of**

directing attention. In seeking *the flow***, we direct our attention upstream into the energy of love flowing into the world.]** Next, our minds bring an 'understanding' to the task… **[Here we now know that the understanding we bring is our understanding of ourselves within our posture of recovery.]** Then our mind must admit that there is more that it cannot understand, that must be experienced. At this point the mind takes on an observing role.

Next, attention goes is to the body, through breathing. Take a deep breath. Let it out slowly. Place your attention on the feeling of your body breathing. **[Know now that exchanging breath is exchanging the energy of life.]** Use your breathing as the window into your body and how it exists in this moment. **[How it exists in relationship with power beyond.]** From time to time the ideas of the mind may come to you. Passively, direct the mind to the notion of *the flow* and ask, what it would feel like, in your body, to be in *the flow*. **[To surrender fully to what power beyond asks of you.]** Allow, the expression of this feeling to seep into your body without allowing your mind to attempt to describe it. Like the feeling of warmth, your body understands it; your mind does not need to be involved. At this point you are imagining it. You are wondering what it feels like. Your body is answering. *The flow* is actually something that your body knows, something it remembers like it remembers how to breathe. There is no struggle. Just breathe and allow the idea of *the flow* to reside in you.

When you have trained yourself even slightly in connecting mindfulness with breath, you will naturally begin to drift into the position of the observer. **[What you are observing is your relationship with power beyond.]** This will happen slowly and without effort. This place from which you are observing is in the direction of Spirit. **[This means that you are looking upstream, in the direction of spirit and potential rather than downstream at results.]** As you are observing yourself in mind and body allow yourself to accept that the vantage point from which you are observing is closer to Spirit than is your normal state of being. Bring part of your attention to the notion that in the universe you are not the absolute power. Bring that part of your attention to your undefined notion of a power beyond. Allow into your imagining an awareness of that power flowing through you into what you are observing. **[Remember, you are observing the energy stream, or the flowing of that energy into the events and objects around you.]**

The feeling for me is like the feeling of being in a room. **[I can amend that now from feeling like being in a room to feeling like I am immersed in energy.]** In the room is my usual self, my mind and my body, as I commonly know them. My vantage point for observation is by the door to the room or a window and I open it to let the power beyond enter. **[I am in the flow of the energy.]** Sometimes I imagine the feeling as light flooding in; sometimes it is wind. The more I have experienced this the more it is simply the feeling of a shift, or a change. **[This is the shift from downstream to upstream.]**

The change is not at one particular point it is everywhere. It is accompanied by the feeling of gratitude. **[This is the feeling of being centered in upstream awareness. It is like having the sun on your face. It is the direction that is directly toward the flow of creative energy.]** When I feel this I move into what I am feeling. This is the feeling of the completion of the envisioning. **[The flow indicates that we are opening to possibility. We are not defining that possibility. In more specific envisioning some definition is possible but in connection through the flow we are allowing the full range of possibility to come to us.]**

Notice that as the process of envisioning unfolds the object of the envisioning disappears. If you hold onto the object, or plan for the results of the envisioning, you will wind up *trying*. This is an unavoidable consequence of holding the object too tightly. **[This is an automatic tendency to return to downstream observation, ego oriented awareness.]** I would never even attempt to convince my mind **[or ego]** of the fact of an envisioning. Envisioning is always about more than was originally intended. **[It is always in partnership with power beyond.]** The object always winds up being just the beginning: the impetus. This is some of the magic. I don't analyze the results of my envisioning. The mind cannot understand envisioning. Analysis seems to set up an unconsciously counter-envisioned intent. To analyze I must also expect the opposite. **[Limitation.]** Instead, I end by observing gratitude purely, without expectation, forgetting that I consciously envisioned at all.

Now, you can understand that to be within the flow is to be in a cooperative partnership with power beyond. You, personally, choose form and content and manifest it within the physical world, but all that is, and all that comes of it, is created by, in, and with, the energy of love, as power beyond expresses it. You are the lens through which the energy flows but not the source of the energy. Thus, we are always within the flow, we are in fact part of the flow ourselves. To perceive this consciously and to surrender to it willingly is to take our partnership closer to the source of the energy and further from the result. To do this is to feel more the essence of the energy and judge less the worldly outcome.

At this point it, if you wish, you may be come to understand power beyond as the creative power or as the power of *your* creator. In this change of wording I would like to re-emphasize that any concept of power beyond includes the fact that it is your *personal* version of power beyond that counts. There is no overall power beyond, because there is no reality to anything "over all." There is no hierarchy of larger than/smaller than. There is only one relationship that, in our individuated physical experience, we feel as our personal relationship. There is no need or mandate or even purpose for either seeking or reaching agreement about our personal versions of this relationship. There only is a mandate for honesty, purity, and clarity. With these essential elements we will find ourselves in oneness, not by effort, or compromise, but by experiencing what is real.

The feeling of separateness is part of our experience in the physical realm. To avoid the hold of ego we must maintain the concept of creator without hierarchy. The creator does what the creator does. Our relationship to the creator is as it is. Assign no relative value to this relationship. As individual human consciousnesses we do not create. Ours is the function of experiencing within the physical realm. Choice over what we experience is given to us. The meaning and quality of our experiences is up to us but we do not create them. This does not make us lesser than the creator nor greater. One person's creations are neither more nor less than another's because separateness is ultimately only part of the illusion. Thus, to move toward the source of creative energy is not to become more virtuous or better than before. All these are concepts that we have left behind as we climbed the pyramid.

From the end of Chapter one:

> The Flow is a state of being where you are in a cooperative relationship with all that surrounds you. Surrounding includes the thoughts surrounding you (mind), the space, objects, and people surrounding you (body), and the energy surrounding you (spirit). Your relationship with all of this I refer to as the flow. In the relationship we seek within the flow the things you need appear to you. The people you need come to you. The circumstances of your day seem to work out. It feels as if you are being given a gift and there is no thought of worthiness or deservingness. There is no obligation. It is simply as if the wind is blowing in your direction. The resulting feeling is gratitude.

You can see now that all that surrounds you is the energy of your creator. All thoughts, all things, all events are composed of the energy of your creator. This energy is the energy of love, though this realization may still be difficult to hold. After all, if the experience is one of death or pain how can this be created in the energy of love? Love is supposed to be pleasant, right? The love of the birth mother is directed toward the nurturing of the children. The love of our life partner is directed towards the sharing of our fullest self within acceptance. Dog lovers love their dogs in part because they perceive that the dog returns that love unconditionally. All these are pleasant experiences. How can it be that the energy of your creator is love if it can be expressed in the form of car accidents, terrorism, child abuse, cancer, or chronic debilitating disease? How can we give ourselves to the flow if the results are not predictable?

First, you must understand <u>fully</u> that there is only one relationship that is real. It is a difficult concept to even think about from within our illusion and even more difficult to accept deeply. When you regard what you perceive to be the suffering of someone else. You are not in an actual, real relationship with that 'other' person. Your relationship with them is no more than a reflection of your relationship with yourself, which is, the relationship between you and your creator. The illusion of separateness that the ego imagines, that there is a sufferer and, separately, you, the observer, is an illusion so alluring that we continually fall into believing it. Even as I write this I hold myself within that illusion because without it there would be no reason to write at all. The illusion exists to provide us with what we are experiencing. We are, in fact, experiencing the illusion because without it there is no experience to be experienced! Outside of the illusion there is only being, all-ness, and the eternal moment that contains all possibilities at once. There is a sufferer so that we can experience it. Suffering seen from this perspective is simply the background required to experience joy. Neither is the better. Both are the same.

This is nothing new. I'm not writing anything that others haven't written many times before, but how does it relate to the here and now, to the suffering in front of us? When I am sitting with a patient who is suffering what is really happening? It depends on the level at which I am experiencing. Or, stated differently, how far into the illusion I have chosen to experience. At the most deeply enmeshed level I may be debilitated by the fear that I may one day be exactly where the sufferer is. At a slightly higher level I may be unconcerned, perceiving that the person's suffering has little to do with me. Higher still I may connect with the person suffering through a sympathetic response feeling part of their suffering not in fear, but with sympathetic love. And yet higher still, I may see that the suffering is a gift to me that lets me know a possibility without having to enact it myself; level after level of your own choosing until I see only the relationship between suffering and joy. Eventually, I come to a place where the suffering and the joy it contrasts are one and the same, that the sufferer and I are one and the same, that this moment of suffering and the next of joy are one and the same. Note that I am not saying anything about envisioning or changing this experience. At this point I am only addressing having the experience in pure form, so that we can come to the balance needed to envision. Envisioning born in the experience of fear will only create more of that experience. Envisioning born in a sympathetic experience only, as in taking on the other's suffering as your own, may only spread the suffering. Pure experience is experiencing the event through all its levels knowing that it is only experience and not a basic truth.

So, my experience of suffering is thus dependent on my level of awareness. Or another way of saying this is, how far upstream or, toward source, I am choosing to experience. Everyone knows how to make a choice. We make choices all day every day. But, we make our most powerful choices so automatically that we are not conscious of the mechanism or the moment of choosing. We can awaken our consciousness in choosing by paying attention to the operation of the choice. By this I mean the mechanism we use when we make the choice. For instance if you put a bell on your left turn signal it would draw your attention to it every time you make a left turn. The choice we make to suffer is similar. We need something to remind ourselves each time we make that choice.

I had a patient who came to me saying that she had become depressed after she retired from her teaching job. She had gained weight and become comfortable sitting on the couch all day. She had developed pain that another doctor had labeled Fibromyalgia, and she had been told she had chronic fatigue syndrome. She seldom felt like she wanted to do anything and she was irritable in her spousal relationship. She didn't know if her husband loved her anymore or if she loved him. She certainly knew that they weren't spending time together.

We did the usual blood work and doctor stuff and everything checked out fine. I began to talk to her about breath and mindfulness. Though she didn't have much energy for change she agreed to try it. I also encouraged her to get out once a day and find something that she felt was beautiful and just look at it for a while. She made an effort to change her diet and often came in angry with herself for one thing or another. Over a series of visits I spoke to her about her life and brought her to the notion of envisioning and the question of what she wanted from her life now.

It was a difficult subject as it is for many patients. Initially, she felt that I was saying that since envisioning implies we are in control of our lives at a very deep level then her situation was her fault. This is such a common reaction and it is so destructive that many people never get over it. Our culture loves to assign fault, and we are very good at it. The fact that fault has no place in envisioning takes some time to digest. This is why even before discussing envisioning I suggest people work extensively with mindful mediation and understand the notion of passively and non-judgmentally returning to intent.

Beginning, as we all do, in whatever the situation was that was significant enough to get us to try something different, the notion of fault seems always to be present. Depending upon our personality, that fault may be directed inward or outward, but it always seems to be present somewhere. And, it is not that causal relationships cannot be defined in any given situation. It is just that this exercise of faultfinding and the holding of the resulting feelings does not help. At a certain level of awareness, quite far from source, fault makes perfect sense. Zillions of human lives have been lived at this level and many more will continue to be lived there.

My patient came to understand that the time and energy she spent assigning fault wasn't helping. Slowly she released her investment in faulting and began to look at what she could do. At this point she was still depressed, on the couch, yo-yoing her weight up and down a few pounds each month. She didn't want to try antidepressants, and in truth her energy was not low, it was simply misdirected. We had been seeing each other once a month for about 6 months. She was having various aches, pains and injuries that kept her distracted. Looked at from sufficient distance she was having a normal life but inside she was preparing for something new.

She developed a breast lump. I found out about this later, since she went to her gynecologist, received a mammogram and was referred to a surgeon.

This took several weeks. Waiting for the biopsy result took another week. She came to see me several weeks later. She was practically glowing with the energy of the flow. The biopsy had turned out to be negative, but that was almost incidental in her thoughts. Instead she talked about the experience as a whole and what it had done to her relationship with her husband. He, faced with the possibility of losing her to cancer, had become very caring and warm. For a time she had received the attention she had been craving from him. In the process of these weeks she had seen him with new eyes, and she had re-identified what she loved in him. It turned out that she loved his independence, his ability to take care of himself, and his willingness to pitch in. She realized that when she had retired while she had expected him to shift his life around now that she was home more, in reality she wouldn't have respected him if he had begun to dote on her. Instead, that would just have given her the excuse to push him away and assign external fault instead of internal. The cancer scare had brought them together, allowed them to reaffirm their love. The negative biopsy result then released their fears.

After she spelled our her story in the first fifteen minutes of the visit I commented that she had done a great job with that envisioning. A confusion came across her face and she asked if that meant I thought she had done it all on purpose. I replied that 'on purpose' is a term relative to a point of view, but that she had surely brought into her life an experience that beautifully produced exactly what she needed. It was even an experience that didn't require lasting consequences. Her confusion started to lift and I added that it didn't seem possible that she, by herself, could ever have designed such an experience, but in concert with power beyond such things are possible. Now the only question left is how she would hold it. I suggested that she could hold it in gratitude.

She smiled, just a little smug, and the next time she came in she told me that she had figured out that the reason she was having difficulty losing weight was because when she was small one of the most important nurturing influences in her life had been her Grandmother. She recounted the feeling of being hugged and picked up by her Grandmother and the fact that her Grandmother had been heavy, pretty much like she was now. She told me how important it was for her to play that role for her own grandchildren and how she had found the part of her that believed that she had to be heavy in order to do it.

Having discovered this she knew how silly it was that she had to be heavy in order to be a nurturing grandmother. Her weight began to come off and while she doesn't choose to be as slim as a model, she is now happy with her physical self. She has become very active and the pains she *suffered* at the beginning of her journey are mostly gone. Occasionally they return and she knows what they mean. Immediately, she opens to her next step.

This patient isn't here to directly cure the ills of the world. Her envisioning is focused on her family and loved ones. Her harmony surrounds her and her family but it also leaks into the collective with all the power of the most visible national figure.

> From deep within the flow desire is known and manifests. To manifest consciously our task is only to know ourselves.
>
> What we perceive (place our attention upon) we draw into our experience.
>
> Grandfather Stalking Wolf; from various times

These are not new thoughts of course. Anyone who has had a crisis of faith has screamed into the dark desiring to know why. One problem comes to us as a legacy of history. Our versions of power beyond have been personified so that we have felt that things were being done *to* us. We have seen our relationship with our creator as having some similarity to our relationship with a neighbor, a father or a mother. In this way when something bad happens we reenact all our feelings from the lower places on the pyramid. We feel that we must be unworthy to be so judged, so bad as to … and insert any unwanted experience. We take on this unworthiness as an identity. It begins to color our unconscious envisioning, and so we continue to experience events that seem to justify our feelings. Yet this is nothing more than a falling from our posture of recovery and returning to the experience of addiction. It is tantamount to the alcoholic blaming the bottle for his problem. It is a misunderstanding of a situation that is clear from a perspective sufficiently far into recovery. The problem is disconnection from power beyond and from our true self. It is never an external substance, behavior or situation.

At Tom Brown's school we often do an exercise that helps us to understand the role of envisioning in our lives. This exercise takes many forms, but is always consistent in one aspect. Tom calls the exercise by many names depending on what the specific object is, but I have come to think of all of them together as *spirit first* exercises.

I taught one of these to my son when he was eight and he taught it back to me when he was eight and a half. We were out walking on a late fall day. There had been an early snow and we were following the tracks of a fox across some low land near where we lived. We had gone out for another purpose, but then saw the fox trail and were seduced into following it. Soon he was ahead of me following the trail. With him in front of me my "dad gear" kicked in for a moment and I noticed that he didn't have any gloves, jacket or boots. Though it wasn't dangerously cold we hadn't really dressed for being outside and it wasn't long before he mentioned that his hands were getting cold.

Let's try something I said. Let's just pretend that our hands are warm. We know what it feels like let's just pretend our hands feel like that and see what happens. He wasn't really cold yet I could see by his red color. His peripheral blood vessels were still wide open. He took off on the trail again as soon as I finished talking. We followed the trail for another half hour before we thought about it again and then I asked him. 'How are your hands doing?' 'They're fine,' he said. At that point I think his hands were warmer than mine because although I had been doing the same thing I have years of conditioning telling me such things don't work. He was able to accept what I said without question.

We have all had the experience of being outside working and there being a period where our hands get cold; often if we keep at it our circulation will open up and warm us, especially if we are being active. Perhaps our pretending just served to bridge this gap. We will always have the opportunity to rationalize our experience. After spirit first exercises there is always a buzz of talk around what could be the hidden but understandable mechanism and or what could have happened by chance alone. This is the argument behind the acceptance of coincidence as random event or as communication from something beyond understanding. Spirit first teaches us to move into our intended form and then let go and see what the experience brings without analyzing what is or is not possible. Essentially this is releasing the results and turning toward the possibilities, that is, turning upstream.

When my son was eight and a half we were out in the same area, but now it was spring. The air was warm and wet and the mosquitoes were in full swing. I was swatting and dodging but he didn't seem to have any trouble. I asked him, "Are the bugs biting you?" He said "No." Since I did not really want that answer and I really wanted him to commiserate with me, I persisted. "Aren't they biting you?" He stopped and turned around. He looked me right in the eye and said. "No, they are not biting me." He looked for a moment longer, and then turned back to what he was doing. I realized that he was stating his reality, and not only that, but I observed that it was true for him. He didn't want to buy into my reality despite my being his parent, and he was willing to be firm about it.

That is the problem with teaching your kids stuff. It won't be long before they are way ahead of you.

There is a difficulty in examining the results of envisioning in your life or in the lives of others. Tom Brown refers to it as the problem of the white winged buffalo. Another way I think of it is, looking for the rewind button. This is the hunger for witnessing a miracle from the outside where you can maintain your disbelief at the same time you are seeing the miracle. But, miracles are made to fit in such that they appear natural. If there ever was a white winged buffalo it would seem to be the most natural thing. There is no way to experience your life and your expectations in one way and then rewind to experience it differently, comparing the two.

This is a consequence of the fact that envisioning is a process of creating your life in partnership with the power beyond. As it says in The Course in Miracles, from the perspective of Christ consciousness, time, the past, the facts as viewed by others, are not a problem. Devine consciousness is such that all events and facts can be rearranged to fit the envisioning. All envisioning will fit without the slightest disruption of your experience of reality. It is not a magic show where the goal is surprise and amazement.

Yet we are hungry for the experience of the unreal. There is a place in us that would like the magically dramatic to occur. We would like to see happen things that are "impossible." Movies are full of these plots. It is as if our ego throws up a challenge knowing that it cannot be met just to dissuade us from believing in envisioning. But, it doesn't matter! Regular unconscious envisioning does not require belief. It just is what it is. The conscious experience of envisioning is not different from all the experience you have had so far, except in your consciousness of it. As I have said, it is not a new mechanism. It is only your consciousness of it, and thus your conscious participation, that can be new.

I know, personally, I have a tendency to want to travel a zigzag path. That is, I envision one thing and then another *different* thing so that I can feel the zigs and zags and know more acutely that envisioning is active in my life. This is my ego seeking control again. It doesn't prove anything and it just makes my experience chaotic. I suspect that most of us who begin to seek conscious envisioning will perform this or some similar tactic until we tire of it. It is the nature of the ego to reassert itself. There is nothing wrong. It is just a stage.

It is clear that in coming into the experience of conscious envisioning the ego is a major obstacle. It is also clear that the ego plays a primary role. Envisioning can neither be done by the ego nor without the ego. The ego is that part of us that interacts with the physical world. It literally defines the world for us. When we are born we are at our most egoless. We look wide-eyed out on a strange new place. All possibilities are open for us and we willingly join in the collective envisioning. As mentioned before, this is even evident in the physical structure of our brains. At birth we have the maximum number of neuronal connections, but none of them have been associated with meaning. They exist as the potential for our ego to develop. As time goes on we use the pathway that represents finding our toes, and we don't use the pathways that are not supported by the smiles of our parents or interesting physical sensations, like the awareness of our spirit. Ultimately, our ego resides in the place between our higher selves and the physical world. One of the pathways that is allowed to fade from awareness is that the ego and the feeling of separation are merely illusions our souls are using to generate the contrast required for experience to feel real. This understanding is not gone, but it is unused. Therefore, in order to conceive of a specific envisioning that has specific relationship to the world, the ego must be in the loop, but not in charge. That's the key.

Envisioning For Others

For some of us, particularly in the beginning and perhaps even always, the flow will be the most powerful and helpful personal envisioning. This is simply because there is no specific object and thus, there is nothing for the ego to grab hold of, nothing to which the instinct to control can fasten. What about envisioning specifically for someone else? What about the ones that our ego says are separate from us. If we can admit that we cannot control others could we envision in relationship with them? Would this be a way for the ego to be utilized that would circumvent its desire to control? Is it possible that the ego might learn to play its perceptive and planning role and then step aside? Perhaps we could do it if the other was sufficiently distant from us so as to seem personally meaningless. There is a large instinct within many of us to help others. It seems to be a true and pure instinct, but it is very important to be sure that the effect of our envisioning is indeed helpful.

To entertain the idea of envisioning for others we must truly think about our relationship to others and what that means. In this chapter we are buying into the ego's notion of separateness and, for the moment, acknowledging that others actually exist. I have mentioned obliquely the alternative, which is that there is no separation and any apparent separation is in fact illusion, but we will return to that later. For now, let's simply accept separation and examine our relationship with others. In specific envisionings it is always essential to understand and accept what already *is* before modeling any ideas about what might be different.

Ask the question: Can I really know anything about someone else, and if I can, how can I know? Constantly, in our normal mode of consciousness we are bombarded by thoughts in the form, "he should," "she should," or "if only they would," or "can't they see that," and all these are followed by an idea that seems to us would create a better outcome than the one we are currently witnessing. Often, these thoughts are born of genuine concern and are well meaning. We really do want to make it better, but, look one step deeper. What is better really? And how do we know?

For thirty years or more we in the US have been living in a culture that protects its children to a high degree. We create safe playgrounds. We regulate for safe toys. We prevent what appears to be unsafe free play. In short, when adults witness children doing something that can be imagine to result in harm, they feel justified in doing something to prevent the imagined outcome. The younger the child, the truer this is. What are the results?

Do we really have fewer injuries? What I have witnessed is that many teenagers crave excitement, and haven't a clue what their limits are. No matter what we do kids will grow up and eventually reach an age where they will seek those limits on their own. Currently, it seems that the age when that happens is increasing and thus the limits, when tested, are more dramatic. It is easier to learn what it feels like to fall when you are learning to take your first steps or falling down a slide than when flying out the window of a crashing car. You may think the analogy is rough, but a rougher one still si that it is harder to learn when you are fifteen what it is to be burned by crack cocaine than to be burned by the ember of a fire while playing at your parent's knee. Insulation from danger doesn't necessarily create a safer outcome, especially when inquisitive humanity is involved.

This is one example. There are many others in the areas of public policy, liability law, foreign policy, etc, but the point is that when we take on the job of influencing what is happening to others we have to consider what the natural course of the events is teaching them. Sometimes, the immediate negative outcome, the one you are aware of and considering preventing, is small compared to the lesson it is teaching. An ethic of envisioning for others can be that if I interfere in the lives of others I am responsible for the effects of that intervention. This means all the effects of the intervention, even into the distant future. If considered in this way, deciding to envision into someone else's process is a little dicier and more care is required. Can you see that the more specific is your envisioning for them, the more you exert specific control, the more responsibility you take?

It is not surprising where this is leading. The urge to control *specifically* is usually the urge of the ego. To hold the ego this close to you, to be thinking in terms of specific what-ifs, is to hold the cloudy lens of the ego to your eye. When you do this, because you are giving your attention to the ego first your envisioning will lack power and have little effect. It is a naturally governing system. Another way to look at it is; when your ego alerts you to potential problems, immediately look once more at the situation but this time through the lens of power beyond. Then rest before you act. There may be nothing required beyond your attention. Your simple awareness of a potential problem may be enough to avert the event. We are not in the habit of thinking that our awareness is actually doing something, but attention is powerful and observing this is, in fact, one of the ways that you can actually witness your envisioning in action. It may be that in a certain situation power beyond requires specific action. From the perspective given by the lens of power beyond you will find that your action, be it a specific intervention or general envisioning, will fit in naturally adding to the flow with no disturbance.

Tom Brown talks about envisioning the weather. Sometimes you just want it to be sunny. Sometimes a storm is ruining your plans. What if it were possible to change that? The weather is not all that hard to change, really, but the consequences of it can be huge. Weather systems are not isolated affairs. If a storm is moved from here to there it may rub up against another air mass and touch off a tornado. If rain is quieted here, it may gather up where it has already been raining and cause a flood. In envisioning you are connected to all the changes in which you have played a role. In order for the envisioning to be successful you have to be ready for that connection. Thinking of this as responsibility is one possibility but I prefer just "connection." I am responsible for my actions but I am connected to the results of those actions even if some of them are beyond my current level of awareness. Remember, the mechanism of the universe doesn't forget and is aware. There is no concept of forgetting in a system that expands beyond time and space. We have the glimmerings of this understanding in the theory of chaos mathematics that states that everything is connected in an incredibly complex but non-random universe. Each change affects the whole, and it is not possible for ego level consciousness to predict all the effects.

So, it is all pretty intimidating. Small wonder it is safer to put aside envisioning and return to normal life. Yet, there is still that yearning. It is partly the ego's natural tendency to desire control and partly the soul's yearning for full expression. We are at a crux in the development of humanity. There are problems gathering in the world that may be too large for political process or mechanical invention to solve. There are changes occurring that are the result of large masses of collective envisioning altering our life-sustaining landscape. No amount of customs inspection seems to be capable of keeping ecosystems separate when the consciousness and commerce of humanity is becoming global.

Remember that envisioning is not a new mechanism! It is occurring all the time. When we take up the notion of specific envisioning for others we are not discussing something new. All the time we are, and have been, unconsciously envisioning for each other. Untrained envisioning naturally reaches its most conscious level in close interpersonal relationships. We have hopes for each other. We have wishes both positive and negative. We think well or ill of each other. On the level we think of as inanimate we imagine all sorts of things, including bigger houses, landscaping, more money. We think "I would like to have a relationship with her…" or "he is hot!" These are thoughts that come with all the sorts of subtext of unworthiness that I talked about in the last chapter. He is hot! But I am not… I would like a relationship with her, but she would never notice me… I would like a bigger house, but I could never afford it. I would like a calmer, simpler life, but I could never deserve that much. Envisioning with many layers of subtext sends confusing signals to the universe and ultimately results in not much happening, but this is the stuff of our collective envisioning. Those among us who naturally have less subtext of unworthiness are sometimes seen as more successful, more forceful, even smarter. Sometimes a powerful individual is not optimistic; shit happens. They are neither conscious of it, nor responsible for it. The effect is buffered by the collective, so temporal association or association in physical location, can be indirect. But this changes when we decide to become conscious of our process.

There is a sensation to being around a powerful individual who operates with little or no unworthiness because this individual's unconscious envisioning is so strong. This doesn't mean that it is good or has the betterment of others in mind. In fact, it might be chaotic but we can still feel the power of just being near it. One way of expressing this is "charisma." Sometimes these individuals are actually just experiencing in their own lesson of taking responsibility for what they do. On the soul's journey, if you can think with the concept of reincarnation for a moment, the soul's purpose may include a very powerful lifetime where envisioning comes naturally. In this lifetime, where the purpose is to awaken to power, envisioning may come powerfully and naturally, but without much control. This life may then be followed by several, or many, lives where there is reluctance to wield this power without perspective and knowledge because there is an unconscious memory of what can happen when such a perspective is absent. These lives will contain less charisma and result in situations where the individual seems to be less consequential, but actually they are working on their next lesson. They are coming to balance with their power. Is it possible that many of us are in this place now? Perhaps our next step into the power of coherent envisioning is coming, but we want it to be conscious, informed and led by divine knowing. If so, we are unconsciously creating a worldly situation of need in which to play out that lesson.

This is a lesson our spiritual leaders have been preaching in various forms. The Apache thought of this as the purification of inner-vision. In the last chapter I defined inner-vision as the voice of power beyond or the voice of your creator as it is heard within you. I told the story of finding the shoes I had lost in the woods. That was an introduction to the use of inner-vision in a most basic sense. Now we can explore another level and you will understand the real need for the purification of this conduit of being.

To be connected to inner-vision during your daily affairs is to be within and remain within the posture of recovery. To consider how you might use your consciousness through envisioning to help those around you, even with the understanding that what you think and see is not the whole story, is to work from within the posture of recovery. It is possible that the suffering you see may not be actual suffering. It could be the acting out of growth and learning. To know this, and yet still consider envisioning is to remain humble and yet not become paralyzed. This is the essence of helping. To do this, simple ego awareness is not nearly enough. Awareness through inner-vision is required, and this cannot be by the slow and methodical approach I explained in the story about my shoes. It must be fluid and integrated; it must come to reside in the depth of your being just as does the actual act of envisioning.

Seeing The Soul

The exercise I use to work on the state of being needed to envision for others I think of as *Seeing the Soul*. First I envision the flow. Whenever I get caught up in thinking that I know what is right for someone or some situation around me and begin to act with insistence or an attempt to convince, thus creating not what I intended but just more of a mess, I realize I have forgotten to enter the flow first. There are times when I spend days having forgotten this essential step. We are all learning. There are no actual mistakes, just times when we are still learning a lesson we thought we knew but didn't really.

So, when I do enter the flow, as I look about, I let this question frame what I am seeing: "What would I be seeing if I were seeing the soul of all that is around me?" I might ask: "What would this person look like if they were experiencing the ideal of themselves?" Instead of witnessing them struggling with the particular lesson they are learning, what if I saw them as having learned not only that lesson but also all their lessons? If I look deep, it is as if their soul blossoms before me. Without the flow my attention will bounce back to what I think they should do. Within the flow I will simply regard the energy and beauty I'm seeing. In this way I have used my attention to attract what might become.

I first began to do this exercise during a time when I was going to the mall. I was living alone and would become isolated and lonely. At the mall I could be around a lot of people that I didn't necessarily have to talk to, but with whom I could experience some community. Admittedly there are a lot of other ways I might have developed meaningful relationships, but it was a great place for the "Seeing the Soul" exercise. It is *so* easy to be judgmental at the mall. Especially for me since I'm not really a shopper, and being something of a nature survivalist guy, the mall environment was clearly out of my norm. It was strange even to want to go there, yet I went and it turned out to be a great teacher.

In the mall it was very easy to tell if I was in the flow or not because without it criticism would engulf me and my mind would just rattle on with the things people were doing wrong and what they should be doing instead. Seeing the soul through the flow made the mall into a totally different place. "Fat individuals" became, not thin or model-like, but exactly as they could be. For some that meant solid and powerful. For some it was willowy and fine. Each became even more individual than their current physical form. Through that vision I could often see the relationship between what they might be learning at this time, where they were along their path of becoming and how they actually were manifesting in the physical dimension.

Often individuals my ego would have thought of as nearly hopeless seemed just one small step away from huge leaps forward. Occasionally, as a person went by, a next step or transition they might take occurred to me. I thought that theses individuals might be poised to make that transition. Sometimes, I simply had the recognition that they were right where they had to be for this moment. The mall became as beautiful as the most pristine forest and witnessing it filled me with wonder and contentment.

You might think that this process didn't really help anyone. Of course, I didn't collect phone numbers and do follow up calls. This is part of the essence of envisioning for the other. It is anonymous. The envisioning is done for the sake of the possibility, and the experience of it, not for the results. It is done for the experience of looking upstream into the energy of creative love and divorcing contact with results altogether. It is done to bathe in the faith that although we do not create the world, we are part of its form and its formation. Envisioning for the other is part of our growth into our greater self and part of our communion with power beyond. This was not a faith first exercise for me because in "Seeing the Soul" I am bringing into my own consciousness my version of what the energy of love can become. The results do not depend upon faith because the result is my experience of the vision not the change in another. If the people I am experiencing do change it is not my doing.

The desires of the ego to *fix* someone don't ever have much hope of fitting into envisioning. Neither does a wish to make someone happy or wealthy. Envisioning is altruistic in the extreme except for the experience of witnessing. People's lives are their own and their journey may not be pleasant in the moment that you encounter them, but I have found that the range of what is possible to witness is wider than I thought. Having people find what they are looking for is possible. Having a person's apparent outlook improve is possible. Having someone ask the question you want to be asked is possible. Having the opportunity you are looking for develop in community is possible. But, none of it is possible if you do not have the patience to allow it to occur in its own time and space. Within the flow, looking upstream, it is possible. Outside the flow you will be considered rude and controlling. It is the difference between going it alone and having your creator as your partner. To my own peril I have tested this extensively.

My mechanism for envisioning others is simple.
1. I begin from the flow always.
2. I bring to mind, through seeing the soul, that which I might envision. This may the next step of growth for the individual or it may simply be giving attention to them in their soul form.

    Sometimes, you might envision for a plant or a forest. Comparing the experience of seeing the soul for non-human entities with that of human entities can be very instructive. Our agenda is much stronger for other humans.

3. I check this idea with my feeling of connection to power beyond through the flow.

    Imagine that you have waded out into a stream where the current is mild but present and that you float a bobber on a string downstream from you. Without letting go you see how the stream and the current reacts to your bobber. Does it swallow it under? Does it jump and hack across the stream chaotically? This will come through as a feeling of calmness or urgency etc.

4. If the flow reacts chaotically I must be willing to abandon the idea immediately and allow the next one to take its place.

    There is no agenda in envisioning for the other. (As we will get to next, if there is an agenda, you are really envisioning for yourself.) If I have difficulty letting any specific idea go, my posture is interfering. I must examine my motives.

5. When the idea has been accepted by the flow I simply let it go as if letting go the string on the bobber. This leaves me feeling the gratitude that is my part of bringing the love of creating into the world.

    It is fun then to watch the effects. Nothing will come out of place. Nothing is dramatic. But sometimes you get to see that there is a difference. It is as if the idea appears unbidden in the mind of the one who needs it. It will work so well that you will wonder if it just happened naturally and if it would have happened, even if you had done nothing. You will never know for sure because it did happen naturally. The process of envisioning is not new just your consciousness of it. There will be no proof except your memory.

At times I have tried to share these moments since they can produce high emotions, but now I just allow myself to feel them. I find that this strengthens me Until people who are on a path similar to your own surround you, this telling will sacrifice your anonymity. It will be as if you are taking credit for what has happened. I know that your urge to shout it out comes only from the joy of being involved, but until people have felt the same for themselves they may not understand. Until then this loss of anonymity is likely to cause an imbalance on your posture. This will weaken your envisioning and ultimately there will be less power in the world. So, take care with shouting about the new world from the rooftops. Sometimes it is best just to smile, and if a companion asks you why you are smiling point out the scene you have witnessed, but leave out your part. The time will come when they ask you what is going on. Then you can tell. Recall that there are no rules in envisioning and no authority higher than you. It is my advice that, when the day comes that your friend notices the coincidences surrounding your company and comments upon it, just say,

"Yeah, it is cool, isn't it." When they insist on knowing, start your explanation at the beginning.

Envisioning Self And Carrying And Agenda

In the beginning, we acknowledged that some of us are motivated by physical, emotional or financial pain. Or we are seeking success that we have not yet attained. Thus, we have an agenda. Can envisioning help us here?

Envisioning self is the most challenging for several reasons. Perhaps the first is that change is holistic. It is easy to see that another person else needs to change. We can readily admit the connection between someone's superficial need for change and their deeper issues, even if we don't know exactly what they are. However, when it comes to our own self, most of us want to bargain with the universe. We want to say that we desire change in this area but not in another one. No matter how small is the part that we hold too dear to allow it to change, it will prevent anything from actually happening because change is holistic. There is no mechanism for partial change, but since we are masters of illusion, sometimes we can convince ourselves that things are different for a while. Soon it will be the same again. Such is the experience of most diets and New Year's resolutions, and most people following the directions of a book, including this one, and professional advice of all forms. If the information doesn't generate experience that the person accepts holistically, the cycle will just continue.

This means that in order to access real change for self we have to be willing to put the whole of ourselves into play. We have to be genuine in our thoughts about change, and we have to be willing to let the change go deeper than we can even know. There is a feeling of risk in this. The risk is felt by the ego and it is symbolic of its illusory claim on your power. However, the risk of opening your heart to power beyond is not real.

The second difficulty about changing self is that in order to change from one experience to another we first have to own where we are. That is, in order to access real change we must first access what is already. We have to accept that we are manifesting what has happened and what is happening now. We have to accept that we are playing our role as co-creator *right now*. It is not possible to engage the mechanism of creation while remaining in denial of the fact that we are using it already.

We do this through the same mechanism that we use to solidify envisioning, through accessing the feeling of gratitude. Thus, we must allow ourselves to feel grateful for whatever is happening right now. This might seem strange because you are entering the path of conscious envisioning with the desire to change. How does that fit with being grateful for the way things are? You may feel that it would be impossible for you to feel grateful for what *is* right now in your life. After all you want to change it! But it is by finding gratitude that we turn our attention toward the flow of energy that is manifesting what we are currently experiencing. Since we are envisioning all the time and change through envisioning is occurring already it is only by acknowledging our unconscious envisioning consciously, by facing its flow that we can begin to envision change. Each moment is independent of the last and the next. What we are looking for is to have future moments that are different from our present moments. The place to work on that, the only place, is now, in this moment where things are as they are now. This is because there simply is no other real moment. And, there is no other fulcrum for real change than by looking directly into the energy of love from power beyond flowing into each moment. When you experience that energy directly, regardless of the specific earthly event or object that is being manifest, the feeling is gratitude.

Contrarily, by disliking or hating the present *wishing* for something different in the future you are just ensuring that it won't happen. If your desire exists in this moment only in the form of a wish it will never become anything more than a wish in the next moment. Some forms of thinking about visioning say that you must have faith that what is vision-ed is already in place. I can see how this might work, but my problem is that I don't work well with faith first. If something is currently absent in my awareness I am not interested in trying to convince myself that it is. This approach just doesn't seem real to me. I need a mechanism and wishing or denying absence only emphasizes its lack. The mechanism of envisioning first accepts the present with gratitude. This gratitude is the power because in giving our attention directly to the flow of creative energy we experience it before it is defined in earthly form. Gratitude disconnects one moment from the next. Without this disconnect the next moment will simply replicate the previous. Gratitude connects the now present moment to envisioning and allows the next moment to be whatever envisioning describes.

Our personal desires for change are deep within us all the time. Becoming deeply conscious allows us to access these desires. Rigorous honesty is required for clarity of consciousness at this level. These deep desires are held in our "posture." Through embodying our request or desire as a conscious posture, as a conscious part of our being, we program it into our next moment. As long as we are engaging the mechanism of envisioning in gratitude thereby truly letting go of the past this programming will manifest in our future.

I will break this down further:

1) You must fully own this exact moment in gratitude. Regardless of the circumstances of this moment you can be grateful for the moment itself. There is experience in each moment. You are alive and you can be grateful for that. In fact, you must embrace this moment just as it is before you can do anything about next. This is the turning into the flow.

2) We carry a posture in this current moment. If this posture is anything other than what we have been learning as the posture of recovery it will contain elements that are hidden

in denial and thus are not accessible to change. These hidden parts will anchor us. We will continue to manifest those same denials and their associations over and over again. Only by becoming fully accepting, rigorously honest and willing to be consciously grateful for our entire self and circumstance can we begin to consciously change.

3) Allow your deepest desire to become part of your posture and to become connected with the gratitude you hold in for the present. Hold these two elements, your deep desire, and your gratitude, in your being simultaneously. Then release desire in all forms and turn to awareness purely. This is awareness as seen through clarity, in full accepting aware of power beyond. Accept the feeling of gratitude into your awareness purely, beyond any physical result. Pure awareness loosens the ego's hold. Gratitude connects the released desire to the energy of creation flowing into manifestation.

4) Allow all of your awareness to remain in the lens of power beyond and remain connected in gratitude. Your desire has now been completely released and you are acceptant of whatever happens.

We must be *willing to be conscious*. We do not have to actually become conscious of every aspect of ourselves. This may be impossible since, in our humanity, we are always changing. We are discovering ourselves in each moment. This self-discovery is good; it is part of our potential to envision because as we discover ourselves in the next moment we play our role in defining that moment. But, our willingness to know ourselves must be absolute. Otherwise, we will remain in the past. The present moment, the seat of envisioning and all power, will remain out of reach.

This is a difficult part of envisioning for self. We would much rather just change specific parts of ourselves and let the rest be. We would like it if we could just be more respected, or just make more money, or just feel healthy. But we don't want to admit, much less be grateful for, the underlying feelings or energies that have made us the way we are now. We have to become grateful for where and who we are! We are alive. We are vital. We are experiencing! This is all that is asked of us by power beyond and we are doing it wonderfully.

Even the most suicidal person I have ever talked to is grateful for being. This is true even in the midst of wanting to act to end this phase of being. They don't want to recognize it, but they are grateful for being in this moment for the possibility of ending it all in the next[34]. Of course, if they allow themselves to feel gratitude, they will connect to power beyond and no longer wish to end their lives in this way. Their ego level will resist self-awareness; the study of this is the science, or practice of psychology.

Connecting your desire and the state of gratitude though your posture, your being, and in the current moment, places the creative forces in play. At this point, you must allow for change by seeking pureness of awareness dropping all the addictions and positions of the ego. It is not that change is difficult. It is exhausting to the mind and body to work so hard to remain the same.

Forming our posture of gratefulness requests honesty of the next moment. The addict at the bottom of his or her experience of addiction finally understands that they cannot go any lower. For a mild addict they may express that they do not 'want' to go lower, but for a serious addict the bottom is defined by there being no place lower to descend, while somehow, not yet dying. In this situation the moment of gratitude finally appears. In this setting it does not look like the kind of gratitude we usually see. This is gratitude born of desperation. It is gratitude expressing that what is can continue no longer. With the formation of gratitude, the posture of recovery forms and the connection to power beyond emerges.

---

[34] The notion that we can end it all is of course suspect but in the experience of disconnect from power beyond there is no sense of continuing beyond the physical. That is, since we have not created ourselves we are unlikely to be able to dis-create ourselves.

The honesty that allows the moment of grateful surrender in which recovery becomes possible, is one of desperation. From here, as desperation fades with the first steps into recovery, gratitude must be maintained consciously. The pyramid, in some form, must be climbed. As long as the connection to power beyond is sought with out reservation addiction is doomed and envisioning will bloom.

Thus it does not matter what change is contemplated: a change of occupation or a change of lovers, a change of diagnosis or of prognosis, an experience of dying through disease or through despair. Finding ourselves alive now, and feeling gratitude for what is, creates the opening. Remaining in the posture of recovery characterized by is how I choose to experience whatever comes to me.

Power

I have used the word power several times. Before we can go further with self-envisioning I have to explain the concept of "power" and its relationship to "force." This work is not my own, but when I came upon it, a great problem I had been experiencing in envisioning dissolved. The book Power vs. Force by Hawkins solved this problem for me with what I have come to think of as Hawkins' Ladder. Thank you very much Dr. Hawkins! The problem was the difference between envisioning for self or others and the notion of just getting someone, including myself, to do what I planned. This is the difference between power and force. To manipulate someone, including yourself, is all about force whether it is done by verbal coercion, by conditional body language, by profiteering, or by grabbing a hold and beating into submission. To assist in the expression of power beyond, and thereby assist all parts of the universe simultaneously, is to live in power.

The difference is not in the superficial observation of what is happening but in the motive and the location of attention that drives the action. When derived from force, combative, subjugating or manipulative actions tend to take place; when derived from power, the actions tend to be subtle, to lead by example, or to extending influence by energy and synergy or by pure spiritual attraction. A person living life from the perspective of force cannot access the feelings, principles or even existence of a life lived from the perspective of power. Nor will they notice many of the coincidences in their lives or be curious enough to pay attention to them or to regard them as lessons. Readiness for envisioning is readiness for power. Hawkins makes this understandable in relatively concrete form. Hawkins details the stages in consciousness that form rungs of a ladder that may be climbed from force into power. He helps to make these stages accessible for anyone who chooses to use them.

I thoroughly recommend reading his book in its entirety.[35] I will summarize the points that seem most important to me for envisioning. The kernel that made the difference for me is that he postulates that consciousness comes in different qualities or forms and that these forms may be ranked from weakest to strongest. This is a hierarchy but not of bad, better, best, rather of the character of experience that accompanies each level. The ranking goes like this: shame, guilt, apathy, grief, fear, desire, anger, pride, courage, neutrality, willingness, acceptance, reason, love, joy, and peace. Further, he postulates that there is a divide in this scheme between courage and neutrality that marks the transition from force to power. Courage is the end of force and neutrality the beginning of power.

What I saw when I read this was a clear and easy way to understand the difference between aphorisms, positive thinking, behavioral psychology, etc, and envisioning. As you

---

[35] Hawkins Power vs. Force Veritas 2004 There are many more concepts in his work than the single element I am using.

have seen through these chapters, we are striving for neutrality regarding our current state, accepting it before applying our tool of reason to define our envisioning, which is then released in love. Only from neutrality can we attain the perspective we need. We must accept what *is* before deciding what might be. Then, through the process of envisioning, we look to find the energy of love within us by placing our attention first upon our connection with power beyond. Through envisioning we come to look at the energy imitating directly from the source. As our attention becomes focused exactly upstream the last structured thought is of our envisioning. Then, that last remnant of reason is released, washed away by the experience of coming into pure relationship with power beyond. This is the moment of feeling ourselves pulled across the chiasm. Until this moment and without this sensation, we would be unable to give up reason, unable to fully surrender the ego. Thus, fully focused upstream we become engulfed by the pure and undefined energy of power beyond. In the timeless moment of experiencing energy, untainted by any remnant of the ego, joy and peace are experienced and these sublime emotions solidify into gratitude. The ego then reforms around our gratitude and life goes on. The results of our envisioning will appear as part of the fabric of creation.

To abandon reason is the last step of faith. I experienced this in wilderness training first in the making of fire, then in trivial moments when the ego is distracted, and then in times of purely experienced need.

You may also look back at the climb up the pyramid and see that it took courage to surrender our pride so that we would be able to discover the underlying desires that conceived and drove our fears and which planted us in grief, apathy, guilt, and shame. With this journey we climbed down into the energies of force. I believe that it is just at the point of courage and neutrality that our attention to coincidence awakens. It takes courage to notice coincidence and think of it as more meaningful than happenstance. And, it takes neutrality to witness and wonder about its meaning without either prematurely assigning a prideful justification or performing a fearful rejection. Thus the place in the map of consciousness, as Hawkins calls it, where we move from exercising force to living in power is the same place where the possibility of conscious envisioning awakens.

At first the difference between force and power may not be evident and yet it is always around us. Someone telling what to do is force. The same person setting an example is power. The military solution is force. Gandhi's method is power. A teacher who says do your homework or you will fail the test is using force, while the one who speaks in a way that makes the homework enticing is exercising power. Nature draws me in with scenes of pristine beauty while the inner city scares me. For me this is the power of attraction and force or fear. This is not because of the actuality of city and woodland, but because of the energy in which I hold my personal awareness of them. When we try to cover our shame with an upbeat attitude, so that we look better to others, we are lost at the weakest levels of force. When we surrender our shame to face our feelings of guilt, even then, during the first steps, we are moving towards power.

When I have fallen from good posture and again found myself at the bottom, when the weight of circumstances has seemed too heavy allow complete surrender, when I have been caught in loops of value judgment I found difficult to break, I have found Hawkins' Ladder helpful. I simply start at the bottom and ask myself, "What about this specific situation makes me feel ashamed?" Perhaps I spoke harshly or I was wrong when I *should* have been right. I ponder it in my mind until I tire. Next, I ask, "What about this situation makes me feel guilty?" and I ponder. I follow that with "What makes me feel apathetic?" I try to put words to each of these, climbing the rungs of the ladder in order. By the time I reach neutrality I find that I have changed, and I no longer feel trapped by my circumstances. Often, the flow rescues me by placing just the right circumstances in my life at the right time, allowing me to do what I can in that moment, to be and do the best that I can. When I am climbing the ladder these are uplifting realizations and help me to climb higher.

For me, climbing the pyramid is a long form. I can use Hawkins' Ladder more quickly in any situation. I can ask myself what sort of consciousness am I living in this moment? Am I feeling neutral or angry, courageous or full of love? There is a curious magic in the order of Hawkins' Ladder. I find that when I do not use the rungs in order, the climb is harder and there is less change in me. It is similar to sanding a board smooth with multiple grits of sandpaper. It is actually quickest and easiest to use all the grit-levels of the sandpaper even though the beginner often tries to skip through them. Just as we could not contemplate worthiness until we found some connection to power beyond, it is not possible to jump from shame to anger or from grief to neutrality, though it is tempting to try.

I memorized the steps in Hawkins's Ladder after I first found it useful. For a while it didn't work for me. Then I realized that I had memorized my order switching the places of grief and guilt. When I corrected my mistake the ladder again worked well. As tempting as it is to take shortcuts, my experience says try Hawkins' order as suggested. Establish a success level before you test your own theories. I'll wager you will return to the order Hawkins chose. Like many of these tools there is an initial phase of skill building. It pays to use the full long form to cement our experience. At this point for me, having used the ladder sufficiently, all I need to do to release from shame is to remember the ladder. It is as if the feelings associated with each level course though me in a moment and its work is done. Like the mindfulness trigger I make sure I review and contemplate the full order often so that when I need it quickly, it is still powerful for me.

Hawkins' work also brings to light the threshold between courage and neutrality. He says that it is the threshold between a life that is focused on growth and expansion vs. a life of pulling in and defensiveness. He goes further to say that this is the energetic threshold between life giving energy and life taking energy. I believe this is also the place in consciousness where coincidence comes to attention. In the language of envisioning this is the threshold where sufficient attention has been redirected from the ego toward power beyond, or when we become aware that we do actually possess two lenses to view the world. At this point we see that the choice of which lens, or energy, we will experience is ours.

When we have taken the leap from courage to neutrality our journey is begun. Climbing the pyramid, in whatever form, will bring us to the next crux, or transition that Hawkins' also describes. This is the leap from knowing envisioning in our minds to the actuality of making that reality come to us. It is the mysterious, magical, step of actual creation that we have been working toward experiencing. It is the answer to the question, "How does this magic occur and what is our role in it?" This is the transition between reason and love. With the tool of reason we develop the idea of our envisioning. We bring that reasoned idea to clarity by seeing it through the lens of power beyond but from here reason itself must be surrendered. This surrender of reason is not the surrender of the ego where we turn from one part of the self to another; from relationship with ego to relationship with power beyond. In clarity, in pure relationship to power beyond, to surrender reason is to surrender the wholeness of self. That is the reaching out across the chiasm. It is the hard step of surrendering finally that can only be accomplished in the experience of the pure loving energy of creation. In essence it is the seduction of power beyond that makes this surrender humanly possible. Recall the many descriptions of the "light" experienced in near death experiences. Always, this light is alluring, welcoming; seductive. When the individual returns to earthly experience the light is remembered and fear is dissolved.

The place of reasoning in consciousness is a very high level. It is well into the constructive energies of power and yet reason is rooted in the ego. Reason is on the logical plane where we believe that we can take the next step by generating a fully formed plan and enacting that plan. Envisioning always must surrender the plan in the end. It is as if reasoning is carried right to its pinnacle for each individual only for the purpose of surrendering it to power beyond.

Hawkins says this of Albert Einstein, Newton and similar giants of reasoning:

> Rationality, the great liberator which has freed us from the demands of our lower natures, is also a stern warder, denying our escape to the planes above and beyond intellect. For those entrained [or, held at] at the level of the 400's, reason itself becomes a cap, a ceiling in spiritual evolution. ["400" refers to a scale of energetic power that Hawkins describes. It spans from 30, the energy of shame to 1000, the energy of enlightenment.] It is striking how many of history's great names calibrate at 499 – Descartes, Newton, Einstein, dozens more. [To transition from 499 to 500 is to accept the energy of love over the energy of reason.] It is a sticking point an enormous barrier; the fight to overcome it is the most common, and frequently the lengthiest, of spiritual struggles. (Power vs. Force, Hawkins pg. 223.)

Remember, there is no hierarchy in the concepts of the art of conscious envisioning. Einstein would not have been *better* if he had made this leap into pure love. Perhaps, in ways that were never written down, he did make the leap. In reading about the lives of the physicists of Einstein's time it is clear that these are some of the most spiritual people among us. They were, and others are today, looking with their own methods to cross this bridge consciously. The surrender of reason into the pure stream of love is the release into envisioning. All of us are right were we need to be. For each of us the question is, "What will we do next?" All of it will be experienced and none of it will be wasted or unworthy.

My own experiences in taking this leap were, again, in the realm of wilderness. Primitive fire making provided many of the first opportunities. Having given myself the task of making fire during my seven year old son's two hour soccer practice I had to leap to find what I needed fast enough in an environment that was new to me. Later in many examples like "my shoes" opportunities came where the circumstances were so trivial as to allow my ego to become inattentive. And finally, there were experiences where need became pure enough to catalyze my willingness to leap. Some of these were in teaching groups where I needed to find a track, or a trail, and my ego had no idea where to look. Others were during solitary experiences where my need was felt physically and was very real.

The leap from reason to love is as large a leap as from courage to neutrality but having recognized coincidence and begun our conscious journey we can come to this leap more consciously. If each rung of Hawkins' Ladder is climbed *in order*, then when the rung of reason is reached and must be surrendered, the platform is prepared and secure for the move into love. In rock climbing we call this a crux move. It always involves letting go and it often takes practice. If you try it one time and fall your reason may insist that the move is impossible; just climb again. Use my brother's Yo-Yo climbing technique until you see your way through.

Creative Mechanisms

Many of us think we know what we want. Some of us are honest enough to be in doubt. The famous joke of the genie in the bottle with three wishes reflects this truth. Only the wise and fortunate wind up better off after their wishes. What is it that we want to envision for ourselves? The simple and obvious human desires, material items, are not good targets for envisioning because they appeal strongly to the ego level. This may be disappointing, but it is useful to understand that desire for things is dependent upon deeper levels anyway. Yes, you can acquire stuff, but think for a moment about what that stuff means to you. A house means security. A car means mobility and flexibility. A boat means fun. It is better to envision security, mobility, flexibility and fun than the specific objects. You could wind up with a house and a mortgage you can't pay, a car that breaks or a boat that sinks.

I have made the point again and again that envisioning is not new. It is not new to us as a whole or to you personally. This means that wherever you are now, whatever your circumstances, you are at this current moment in your trail of envisioning. If your boat is sinking ... that means something. If you are sitting on the sideline wondering about a more engaged life, that means something. If you have been up and down several times and you are tired of it, it means something. If you are involved in the thick of it enjoying everything and looking for your next grand manifestation of yourself, that means something too!

Now, I need to explain a concept from another great book. I am very grateful for all these authors who have had the courage and generosity to put their ideas out where I can find them. The book is: <u>The Path of Least Resistance</u> by Robert Fritz,[36] and again, I am picking out only one concept from a book rich in clues. I advise reading the whole book, but the idea that meant the most to me was the concept of linear vs. oscillating creative mechanisms. Fritz studied the difference in process between people who were considered to be creative and those who weren't. Many creative people do not think of themselves as creative. When asked to say why they have been able to create they say that they are persistent, or that they had no choice, but what Fritz noted was that uncreative people used a fundamentally different process in their thinking and action than creative people. The difference wasn't in the people themselves but in the mechanism they naturally employed.

I will explain the two mechanisms in a moment, but first I want to alert you to the fact that the prime difference is just what we have been discussing in envisioning. It is all about how you hold the motive principle. Do you want fun or do you want a boat?

Oscillating mechanisms are the most common. Dieting represents an easily understandable oscillating mechanism. The motive for many people who are dieting is to lose weight. The reason they might state for the fact they are heavy is that they are always hungry. This feeling of hunger and the desire to lose weight are in opposition to each other. Imagine a pendulum. When the pendulum is on one side the desire to lose weight is accomplished; with the other swing the need to satisfy hunger is accomplished.

The motive is the goal, loss of weight or hunger, but the power that moves the pendulum is *will* power. This is the attraction to the goal symbolized by the distance of the pendulum from neutral. Having gained weight a person will have garnered sufficient will power to begin dieting. The sensation of hunger is relatively satisfied while the desire to loose weight is not. This will bolster the will power to diet. The person will eat less and begin to lose weight. As the weight

---

[36] R Fritz <u>The Path of Least Resistance</u> Berrett-Koehler, 1999

comes off, the desire to lose weight will become more and more satisfied lessening will power to diet while the feeling of hunger will become more present. Eventually, the person will be on the other side of the pendulum's swing and the will to diet will be gone, replaced by the desire to satisfy hunger.

I tell this story as if the person hs never dieted, and as if there are no other psychological energies in play. In the case of dieting this is seldom the case but it still illustrates how one form of will power when set opposed to another form of will power always brings about its opposite. This is because will power is not an infinite source of energy. Eventually it will run out. It is not actually a power at all it is a force. It would be more accurate to say the force of will. Fritz found that creative people didn't work with force of will.

Instead creative people used a mechanism independent of will power, one that from my perspective is connected to the infinite source of power beyond. He called this the Linear Creative Method. I will paraphrase his example. A composer is writing a piece of music. He or she has a feeling or atmosphere that they have imagined. It is held in an almost formless state, but their attention is irresistibly drawn to it. It is as if they are seduced by this as yet amorphous result. The composer takes pen to page or fingers to instrument and begins to compose. A few notes are played. Now the composer reflects and asks am I closer to my feeling, my atmosphere, or further from it? If he feels closer, the notes stay. If not, they may provide a clue to the next direction. He plays or writes again.

This may take place physically or may be all in the mind of the composer but the mechanism is the same. There is a dream about what could be. A step or two is taken. An observation of that step is made and the question is asked; am I closer to my goal now or further away? An observation is made and then there is passive and non-judgmental return to the process. This is a re-seduction of the goal. Does this sound familiar? First there is intent, then a step toward, then an event, followed by observation of the event, and passive and non-judgmental return to the intent. The more value judgment is imposed on the mechanism, the more the result of the observation, closer or further, is related to the value of the composer, rather than the process of composing, and the more difficult it becomes.

The more value relates to the success or failure of the project, the ultimate worth of the composer, the skill of the composer, or anything besides the descriptive observation of the event, the more time and struggle it takes. There is a subtle difference between observation and judgment; observation doesn't take sides or impose worth, judgment does. If courage, pride or anger enters the process from the lower regions of Hawkins' Ladder it will contain judgment and it will hinder the process. If desire, fear, guilt, apathy, or grief, enters it may stop the creative process completely. The more the mechanism of observation can focus on neutrality, willingness, acceptance, reason, and love etc. from the upper levels of Hawkins' ladder the more the process will thrive to completion.

When linear creative mechanism is working well there is a feeling that almost overcomes the individual creating. When the goal is becoming closer and thus is becoming clearer, when the momentum is building and the seduction of the energy is strong, it is an upstream event. The composer, the artist, is facing the creative energy of being and that energy is flowing through him or her into the project. The feeling is consuming and artists are often thought of as reclusive or self-centered. Such a person may be hard to have a relationship with. They may seem always to be in love somewhere else. Or if the project loses its focus, they may become severely self-critical. Will power simply isn't in them. To keep driving from personal will is foreign to them. If they cannot regain the seduction of the project, they may dip into depression. In the abandonment of the process, or in casting around to reconnect to it, anger may rise up. In romantic stories this generates great plots and is told as if it is an essential part of the process, but it is not. It is the unconscious aftermath of the process dissolving. Sometimes an artist will attempt to drive the process with ego-oriented force of will. This will destroy the mechanism of linear creation, and in unconscious processing it may take a period of emotional upheaval before the artist returns to the linear mechanism that is most productive.

Having completed a project the artist may feel adrift since nothing can replace the high, the connection to source, they have felt in their creative moments. This up and down effect in the lives of creative people has been recorded through history. It is connection with the source through sublime expression and then disconnection until the next experience presents itself. Artists often don't feel in charge of their next project. It is as if they are waiting for their muse to return. This is why they say that they don't have a choice. The mechanism is simple though. It is the unconscious application of it that is problematic.

In conscious envisioning we are essentially learning conscious creativity. We are learning to connect consciously to the source of power beyond, but when the object of creative intent is the self there is the most opportunity for confusion. To see the self as sublime is sometimes difficult. The seeing the soul exercise is much more difficult with the self. It is fraught with all kinds of judgment that represent all of the struggles of the climb out of ego domination. This is why, along the path of becoming conscious in envisioning, climbing the pyramid is inescapable. Envisioning others is much simpler. Selfless service is a more traveled pathway to spiritual experience. The more distant the other, and the more anonymous the envisioning, the simpler it is. It is hard to set in place an oscillating mechanism with a person or plant that you know you will never see again. Even a suggestion that you may see them again introduces some difficulty because you may, in the future, become aware of the results of your envisioning. What if it didn't turn out well? What if things got worse? What if it succeeded? Is it your fault? Is it to your credit? What if what if.... This can become a fountain of value judgment.

Stay in linear creative mechanism. There is no fault and no credit. The individual who has been successful in many projects neither basks in his glory nor glooms in defeat. More often he is off being seduced by the next project. What if the result wasn't what you expected? Observe, and envision again. What you see as failure may not be. Acknowledge the perspective of a power beyond your own level of understanding. Be humble and know that you cannot truly see the expanse of another's life. You are very lucky if you can come to understand your own.

As you begin conscious envisioning the debate between oscillating and linear creative mechanism will become loud in your awareness. If you remain in oscillation, you will become desperate and retreat to non-awareness where no envisioning will be available. Just as with all the other steps on this journey it is not the actual envisioning of self that is difficult, it is the preparation for it. If you are standing in the flow, in wonderment of the energy you are feeling, envisioning for self will become part of that flow. It will be completely natural. Your innermost desires are not a secret to the universe. They are known and operating all the time. If your envisioning to date hasn't brought you what you think you desire it is because your inner-self and your outer-self are not in synchrony.

Remember, your soul sent you on this journey and is accompanying you every step of the way. There is nothing amiss, nothing is actually tragic, but there can be a lack of awareness between levels. The deep spiritual levels can be motivating the more superficial physical levels to wake up. The deep levels may be willing to sacrifice everything in order to accomplish this awakening. This process can be unsettling or painful. Ego denial is incredibly strong. It is that strong because we made it that way on purpose. It is up to each of us individually to unmake it. There is no other way. If there were we wouldn't be who we are.

Slowly, as the collective evolves, this process will become easier, more known and more accepted. We, you and I, can wait until then. But, I suspect that if you are still reading you are not waiting. You are the artist being seduced and you are way beyond the point of no return. It is your journey to lead the collective this time.

An Example of Envisioning for Self

Imagine that you have cancer. Or, if you really do have cancer I am sorry for your diagnosis, but not for the dramatic imperative your life has given you. Begin with the flow and know that your cancer is part of your flow. It is not a mistake you have made or something that is being done to you from the outside. It is simply an event in your life. Attach no value to it. It is not bad luck. You may not remember having chosen this turn in your life or you may. You may discover the decision point in the process of your journey or you may not. It doesn't matter. You are where you are now like a point on a map. It is descriptive only. Certainly, there are strong emotions attached to that location, and the free expression of those emotions may be part of the experience, but they are neither good nor bad. They simply are, as you simply are.

I can imagine that this is hard to read. Easy for him to be so dispassionate! Let him try it when it is his cancer! I believe I did mention that envisioning for self is the hardest. Positive thinking, slogans and affirmations, or some imaginative imagery of your immune army attacking tumor cells all sound pretty reasonable next to non-judgmentally admitting that this cancer is a part of your life's creation. Let alone the thought that your anger is just an emotion associated with a location in experience and not something more vital about the unfairness of reality! I am with you. I really am. Positive thinking is powerful. Affirmations are ok. I like imagery. I think it is cool and does help. Taking up envisioning in the face of a scary diagnosis like cancer is nearly as impossible as it gets. You have only one advantage. Your need is real. It's as real as your next breath. This is your key.

Starting with entering the flow as always let your cancer be part of that flow. Let all the icky impossible consequences of having cancer into your flow. Let all the rich emotions, the fits of terror, panic, anger and desperation be part of your flow. Breathe it in. The tendency to be in denial half the time, if you are not feeling ill, is real too. It is also part of your flow. Feel it all and let your need grow from it. Need is a basic emotion, but we do not feel it purely very often. We quickly attach it to some object or some event, such as "I need a car," or "I have to cook dinner," but you have the opportunity to tune into your need purely. Yes, you want to live. You want to see your children grow and have children of their own. You want to spend more time with your spouse or do the things you haven't done. All these are desires. What you are feeling when you let yourself be quietly in the flow with your cancer is real need. Let yourself focus in on that need and feel it purely coursing through you. The flow of the river of your time, this life, has become the flow of this need. To let your self really feel it is powerful, overwhelming, magnificent. Let yourself feel it in every moment. It is much more than we ordinarily feel. It is a gift of your situation. It is an honor.

This is not a sit down envisioning. It's not a few moments you set aside. It is not something you do and then go back to being normal again. Normal is gone now. You have cancer. You are in the fight for this physical life. If you live you will be a survivor. Nothing will be the same as it was. If this life ends, you will be journeying on and what is normal here will be disqualified. If you take the journey fully you will have won. You will have done what you came to do. When I said part of me envied addicts because they are in a do or die situation, I wasn't lying. We are all in the same situation. Our time is limited, but when someone tells you that you have cancer they set the clock in front of you and you start to feel it ticking. The end becomes focused and personal. This brings envisioning for self to awareness as it actually is. It is your life in this and every moment, and the key to living it consciously it is need.

This is the scary part. It is the part we want to remain in denial of. Few among us are good at asking for what we truly need. Some are good at asking for what we want, but need is another matter. Generally, we keep our feelings of need at a distance or safely buried in layers of denial. A diagnosis of cancer will change that. It will begin to purify your experience of need.

If we are unable to bury need in denial, the next best thing is to attach it to something convenient and off target. In this way we can feel an intense need for something outside ourselves to change. This gets the focus of need outside of us where we can view it as separate. It is less intense in this way and in average life this works fine. We can spend years trying to change our spouse or saving for a house or a bigger toy. Children are great repositories of our need because it feels particularly legitimate camouflage our own needs as our children's needs. There are an unlimited number of ways that we contort ourselves to avoid the pure sensation of need. And yet, when it comes to envisioning for self, pure need is the juice. Feeling the pure sensation of need awakens the authentic connection. There is no way to be dispassionate about ourselves. We can hide. We can be in denial. We can say to others that we do not matter, but it is all smoke to avoid feeling our need acutely and purely.

Breath training can come back to us here. When you are doing the pulse timing part simply stretch it out too long. There is a sensation that goes with air hunger that is very similar to pure need. The only difference is that air hunger is attached to the object of needing to take a breath. Imagine that sensation purely and you are getting to what I am talking about. When you can feel this sensation clearly and strongly in association with your cancer but without an object popping to mind you are getting there.

When that feeling has become pure enough, and only you can tell when that is, focus it on your cancer. Do this by holding the idea of your cancer and the feeling of pure need together and ask if this cancer somehow gets you closer to satisfying your need. Do this non-judgmentally. It is possible that your time is over. You don't like leaving people behind but it is possible that you have accomplished what you came for and it is time for you to move on. There is a relationship between your need and your cancer because the unconscious flow of your life has led you to this moment. This is a fact. You are where you are. Allow the acceptance of that to penetrate more deeply than it ever has before.

There is a deeper honesty to be found and when you find it, because you are alive, because you are the creator's magnificent offspring, you will also discover your path whether it is to live or die from this life. The creator has no mandate on the duration of your life. Your soul, your spirit, your connection to power beyond and power beyond itself all exist in a place beyond time and duration. You may have the time you choose. Within the connection between your pure need, which is this current life manifest, and the cancer, there is a relationship that is being satisfied. There is also the path to satisfying that need purely, without the object/experience of the cancer. It is likely that understanding this pathway to your next moment will be totally beyond words or any ability to express, but this is the cancer's reason for being. It is to bring this awakening of pure need to your experience and to tell the story of its relationship with your life. Every moment of your life has led to this place, this manifestation of now. The satisfaction of this relationship is your only reason for carrying the cancer with you from this moment to the next.

The release will be simple. The need flowing through your life will not cease. You will remain connected to it more strongly than ever before. If you so choose this connection to need is the power of becoming a survivor.

The Dynamics Of Need

We have now come full force to the subject of need. What is this stuff, need?

Best wishes, instinct, and the divine guidance of inner-vision will work for envisioning everyone but you. For envisioning self, need is the only thing that works. And, it has to be purified need. Need plus any impurity, any worldly thing associated with the need, makes it just desire. To desire something is to empower its absence. There is no power to obtain or create change in the force level energy of desire, but there is in the power of pure need because this is the purely expressed energy of the creator.

This is why, in our ordinary experience, need is instantly attached to an object. If the power of pure need is unleashed, the ego know it can no longer be the ruler of conscious attention. In ordinary consciousness the notion of need expressed without any object even sounds funny. How can you have need with out needing something? Maybe it is possible to feel need without knowing what you need, but you must need something. Right?

Many truths in the realm of spirit exist in paradox when viewed from the perspective of the ego and physical life. We are one and yet we are individual. We are of a unity and yet we experience our individuality. We are mortal yet we are spirit and exist beyond the field of time and space. The only true moment is the now and yet we experience the past. The world experiences war, famine, disease and pain yet it is composed of love. These things make your head hurt because they are paradoxes. Yet, when I smell a paradox these days I look closely because I have found that there is a spiritual truth to be uncovered. It is as if the paradox points the way out of the ego's realm. Thus, it is need, without object, that exercises the true power of envisioning.

How do we access this sort of need from here, from our physical realm? We are spirit, but we think with the ego's equipment. Imagine that you are in a state of pure spirit. All of time is visible to you. All possibilities are laid out as if on a table. All experiences of having and of not having are present at once. All the connections and interconnections are clear at once. In spirit you are able to observe this whole dispassionately. Because you are aware of all things, nothing is closer or further from you. Nothing is more intense or less intense. Though you are not the totality of everything your awareness is evenly spread out. That is, until you hear the voice of unity, of power beyond, directing you. Power beyond is asking something of you even while you still exist purely in spirit form. It is asking you to sacrifice your continuity with the unity, your view of the wholeness of spirit, in favor of the intensity of individual experience.

This is no sacrifice really. From your perspective of existence in spirit you understand this implicitly. There will be a return to oneness and unity. You cannot actually separate from unity. Time is a construct of localizing your awareness and doesn't really mean anything to you. There is no downside to accepting individual experience. There is only the opportunity to do this action and from the knowledge of this possibility a certain feeling is born. It is the first feeling that is not the totality of love. The feeling is in alignment with the energy of love flowing from the unity, and the feeling is the request from power beyond for you to experience your individuality. In spirit you know yourself to be intimately a part of the unity and of its energy. You may access any part of it you choose. In fact, the only difference between you and the power itself is that it is the whole and you are a part. Experience is only available to you as a part because you can experience yourself in relationship to *other* parts. Experience as such is not actually available to the whole. You understand this from spirit in the eternal moment in which the unity exists, and with that understanding and from the request, the motive feeling develops. This motive feeling is the feeling of need. In its pure form it is the request of the unity, of power beyond. It is the request of the whole to the part.

This feeling of need propels us into life and becomes constituted into all the details that make up a life. The ego does its job of keeping our attention focused here by attaching the feeling of pure need to various objects and events. This makes those objects and events into things of importance to us and makes us fearful of losing them and on and on it goes. Consciously and unconsciously we feel need at all the levels of our being. From it we manifest our physical selves. And, if we so choose to manifest ourselves consciously, we must regain conscious access to this motive principal, pure need. It is the only way to get our hands on the steering wheel. If we are not working with pure need we are always going to be dealing with energy that is already at least partially formatted, partially defined. When we are looking for a clean break from the past, when we want to choose something actually different, pure need is the energy we must use. It is the love of our personal relationship with power beyond that is given to each of us individually. It is and remains what it was while we were in pure spirit form. It is the request of the whole to the part seeking experience. Thus, need is the essential connection to power beyond at the individual level.

The study of wilderness survival is helpful in the process of seeking the purification of need. In modern society our egos have attached the energy of need to thousands of things. In society, it is very complicated, but in the wild our needs become more basic and simple. Tom Brown calls these the *sacred* needs because they are needs that are so basic that they approach the realm of spirit. Shelter, water, food and fire; these are the four sacred needs. Without them the life of the ego and the illusion of experience will not continue. Learning to satisfy these needs from the purity of wilderness is a special experience that teaches us the experience of pure need.

Once again I can tell you about that experience, but in so doing you will only know about the experience. The lesson requires the experience itself.

Tom Brown's books are full of stories where the need for one of the basic four of survival became so acute that some barrier was surmounted and a new experience was attained. I will leave you to read his stories directly or attend his school and listen. For myself the study of survival in wilderness didn't approach the ragged edge of death quite so often, but it had some of the same qualities. For me the study of survival has always been secondary to the study of awareness. I desire to survive because I need an expanding field of awareness. This is how it feels to me.

Last year, while camping with friends, I was digging the small roots of Trout Lily for a tasty addition to the evening stew. I wasn't particularly starving, but I was hungry and the food would be welcome in the evening which was still hours away. I was however ravenous for the experience that I imagined had occurred hundreds of years ago when human beings lived in tight groups and harvested their food together as a community project. Trout Lily is one of the foods that I imagined would have been harvested in this way. It is a small pea sized root that in early spring puts up a single leaf. It is right at the edge of being worthwhile, not because of its taste, which is wonderfully delicate, but because of the time it takes to gather and the relative calorie value obtained. You have to find a location rich enough in the plant and easy enough to dig, but also, it seemed to me, that there had to be some other level of secondary gain as well.

Although I was in the woods with six or eight people, we tended to separate during the day for our own experiences and come together at night. I had been able to talk one companion into the notion of harvesting Trout Lily. This was fine company in the reality of our age, but I was hungering for what it might have been like thousands of years ago. I found that the Lily roots were biggest out in the open under the sun. Also, it was best to look for relatively dry sandy areas where they were easy to dig. These areas tended to be beautiful, comfortable, warm, and bright. It was all very welcome in the cool of spring when rains come often. At one point, I was feeling my need for expanded awareness, and was simply allowing it to enter my state of flow as I was digging the roots. From that flow I began to feel as if a tribe of people surrounded me. Though all was silent except the wind and the digging of my single physical companion, it was as if I could hear children playing. Using the ego's sensing apparatus of eyes and ears I pretended I could see, hear and feel what it was like to be within a tribe, on a warm spring hillside, digging Trout Lily. There was a seductive passion in this experience that helped me to connect to it fully. I dove into this passionate connection hungry for the experience of a reality different from my own. In the experience of pure need as it flowers into a representation, it releases into passion that catalyzes the connection making it feel real. From my experience I realized that this was the secondary gain. For myself, envisioning in this way the gain is the feeling of that passionate connection, the energetic fulfillment of experience. For the Trout Lily it was that this was a food that could be gathered from the area exactly where the tribe wanted to be on a sunny spring day because it provided the most enjoyment available.

To me this is the shelter of the tribe. This is the feeling of inclusion that my pure need was pointing toward through my envisioning. In this way, by allowing the feeling of pure need to infuse the flow for me, I was led toward the experience I sought. There was no requirement for me to define that experience in advance. Because I did not the experience was able to come to me naturally and through my passion penetrate deeply. My awareness actually did expand to know what I had craved and my whole experience was enriched. The experience remains with me today.

I did not tell this story to my physical companions that evening. We shared the Lilly bulbs and laughed and told other stories of the day. My energy of need flowed into the group and combined with theirs and we shared a grand evening. The energy of my experience was fulfilled.

These experiences are small. There is no white winged buffalo. They fit into our lives naturally if we let them. They are the stuff of real need entering our lives and shaping our experience. When a dramatic experience comes along, like the diagnosis of cancer, or an automobile accident, when the events around us seem to be making no sense, and coincidence is being overwhelmed by calamity, it is well to have practiced sensing pure need in smaller situations. The big ones are driven by the same energy. There is only the energy of love given to each of us individually expressed as need. When a boon or a calamity occurs, we must ask the same question: What is the experience my true self is looking for? This is the doorway to the expression of your pure need into any particular form. Without acceptance of the currently manifest form and without understanding the attachment of your need to that experience the purification of that need cannot occur. The manifestation of the energy of your need must backtrack[37] to its origin beyond all attachments or change will remain inaccessible and the experience will simply unfold as it was unconsciously designed. Passion is the key to this backtracking. When did passion become activated? What is keeping it activated now? How can that passionate connection to essential energy be maintained while the experience is allowed to change?

Again, to change such an experience does not require that you somehow grab hold of it and do something dramatic, though that is what the ego wants. Rather, change at this level requires that you surrender to the experience enough to accept it. This often requires that you forgive yourself for it. Surrender is the right word because it is acceptance of what you prefer not to accept under compulsion. The feeling of compulsion comes from your ego and its unwillingness to lose control. It is, but does not feel like, a release into freedom. From the side of the current experience it feels like waving the white flag and giving up. Only having done that can you to turn your attention upstream to the energy that is feeding it and realize the freedom. No amount of effort will accomplish this, only the surrender of effort.

This surrender business remains difficult to tackle head on. In his book Ishmael, Daniel Quinn[38] characterized humans as beings who cannot put something down without picking something else up. To enter into pure surrender is that kind of act and it is

---

[37] Hence the connection to animal tracking classes: The experience of backtracking a vague animal trail, days old, when the prints are fading from conscious view, feels just the same.

[38] D Quinn Ishmael Bantam; Reissue edition (May 1, 1995)

difficult for us. This is the role of gratefulness. Gratitude is the solidifier. It is the thing we pick up when we put down whatever it is we are surrendering. This changes the task from something nebulous to something specific. To become grateful for an experience is at least concrete enough to be considered. It may seem difficult to find gratitude in some experiences but gratitude for pure experience itself is the key to the pure need fueling the experience. This pure need is the gift of our individuality that we can always be grateful for.[39]

In summary we are delivered to need when we begin to consider envisioning for self. The feeling of need, purified, is the request from our personal creator for experience. Any and all specific experiences fulfill this request, but our individuality may prefer one experience to another. When this control is handed to the ego rich physical experience is accomplished but because of the ego's mechanism of denial it can become uncomfortable. Our task of awakening to conscious envisioning is the task of regaining the direct experience of attention, beyond denial, while still accepting the ego in its assigned role. The ego is useful in describing what is happening in the world around us but not in defining it.

When we come to the conscious task of changing our experience the purification of need is the fulcrum. We must reach for that purity of need before

---

[39] Many people suffering from addictive disease, eating disorders, depression, will state that they no longer want their individuality. Through suicidal intentions they claim that they no longer want to exist. But, when I test this by ignoring their individuality or truly get to their beliefs about non-existence, so far I have always found that it is the quality of their experience they want to escape from, not the presence of experience itself.

form, before we can change our current experience. Once purified, we can understand the connection of our current experience to pure need by holding our experience and pure need side-by-side in fully conscious, non-judgmental, attention. Nothing derived of the ego can be present in this holding and because of this the specifics of experience become less distinct. Once our experience is understood as a feeling or a presence beyond words, then we may exchange what we are experiencing for what we are envisioning. The object of our envisioning must fulfill the feeling of the need completely on a level far beyond words. To do this the envisioning must flow from the source of pure need, which is our connection to power beyond.

Holding the connection to pure need and filling our awareness with it will disconnect the old experience because it is too specific and because we are no longer passionate about it. Instead, we are filled with the energy of need in its pure form. Then our honest, humble, non-judgmental connection to power beyond will connect the new envisioned experience to the need.

Imagine that we are holding our current experience physically with both hands. We are passionately involved with it and this is symbolized by the fact that we are holding it tightly with both hands. Through the process of connecting purely with power beyond we notice that there is an energy flowing around us. We let go of our experience with one hand and reach for the energy instead. Our experience still hasn't changed but we are less connected to it. We are hanging on to it with one hand. Our ego is telling us that if we let go--- we don't know what might happen. There is fear and we revisit all the difficulties while we were climbing the pyramid, but eventually we learn to let go and hold the pure energy of need with both hands for the moment of transition. Then, and only then, can we reach for something new. Before this moment of immersion in pure need we would only reach for what was previously known. Unlike our experience of envisioning with the flow where what is required is the we turn our attention purely into the flow. When envisioning for self, because we are so involved we must instead reach for purity of need, the pure command of the creator for experience, in order to disconnect from what has been and be able to experience envisioning of something truly new. However, just the same as when envisioning the flow. When we do let go to purity of need and experience our relationship with power beyond without any agenda or personal desire we experience the creative energy of love in its pure form. This is reaching across the chiasm separating what is from what will be and it is the experience of love and joy. Once again this feeling, too powerful for sustained human experience coalesces into gratitude.

Power comes from allowing the sensation of pure need to blossom fully and engage passion. Passion bridges the acceptance of the new experience as happened through the passion I felt when the villagers harvesting Trout Lily surrounded me. Then, we let go into gratefulness. This move to grateful appreciation of experience is always the endpoint of envisioning because within it is the humility that acknowledges that from human perspective we do not see the whole. We know deeply that there is always more to an envisioning than we see and this wholeness is left forever to power beyond.

Expansion Of Self

There is just one more tool we need in our bag to call it complete at this stage. I believe the lessons of Spirit and awareness continue forever, but books do not. After this point my journey seemed to round out and I rested for a while. This last lesson I came to think of as "the expansion of self."

The first stage of the lesson, essentially the starting point, is the "extension" of self. It is a beginning to break down the experience of self vs. other that it had been the ego's job to create. Here is a story to illustrate.

> One day as I sat in my bathtub I wondered where, outside my window, the deer were. I could not see them. My window had only a nearby view. Yet, I had two great friends who were outside. I thought that my two friends' vantage points would surely take in the evening feeding grounds of the deer. I closed my eyes and asked my friends what they saw. My friends are two great pasture oaks. Each stood in a corner of the field adjacent to my home. I asked them if they saw the deer. Of course, they didn't answer in words, but rather, it was as if I began to see from the tops of their branches. From there I saw where the deer fed. There was little sense urgency or anything unusual in my connection with the oaks. At times it seems that the world of spirit takes the opportunity of the right mix of casualness and intent to show us how the real connection feels. Perhaps my intention was pure because I had not logically debated with myself before beginning. Perhaps, because my communication was too spontaneous to allow thought, I caught my ego sleeping for once.
>
> Having seen the deer I threw on my clothes and ran out into the field. Each Oak had showed me a location but not the same one. I wanted to know which if either was correct. Evening was falling into dark as I crept forward.

I didn't want to disturb the deer before I saw their location. They grazed just where I expected them to be as told by the first oak. I watched amazed, and thanked my friend who now looked over my shoulder. In the beauty of the deer I had become completely satisfied, and had forgotten all about the second location. As darkness fell I began to return home taking a different route. To my astonishment I disturbed a second family of deer that had been grazing just where the second oak had shown them to be. I remembered my intent had been to ask the oaks exactly where the nearest deer were. I had asked each of my Oak tree friends separately. Naturally, since a different group of deer was nearer to each of the oaks they had given me different answers.

In this experience I allowed my awareness to extend to the awareness of the oaks. You may question the presence of awareness in oaks, but that is not the point. The point is that through the extension of myself I attained an awareness that was useful to me. I could have just soaked in the hot water, luxuriating in my individually, as I have done many times, but in this experience I chose to extend myself and found another barrier fall away. At the time I clearly thought of the oaks as separate from me and yet within the *character* of the communication 'it was as if I began to see from the tops of their branches' there began a cracking in the illusion of my individuality.

The extension of awareness is an interesting tool to use when lost in the woods, or when looking for a specific plant or track. Once this barrier is broken, a whole field of awareness opens and becomes a vibrant part of life. In the past, when confronted with a patient I didn't understand, I would persist in my logical questioning. I would find relatives or dig out records. Having found the ability to extend awareness, I am now more apt to seek understanding by seeing that which I should not be able to see. Then, as I ask my questions to confirm the impressions I received through extension, I find I am often correct or that the question now opens the door to the understanding that I need.

Somewhere along the road, I'm not sure exactly where or when, this extension of awareness gave way to expansion of self. This is a posture where I am not just receiving information. I am becoming larger. There are perhaps stages to this: imagining what it might be like to be someone else, extended awareness, projection of awareness, projection of presence, eventually leading to the recognition of self as inclusive rather than exclusive. The evolution from extension to expansion is a natural part of the process of becoming aware in envisioning. At first the other seems tangible, but soon the barriers are not so firm. At the point of expansion, envisioning for the other becomes envisioning for self. What had seemed to be outside is now accessible from inside. The need of the individual has become the need of the whole. The illusion we used in envisioning for the other is now eroded away. It is replaced by expanded levels of self where, without effort, small internal adjustments expand into the flow.

The ego self is but one layer of the whole self. It is one shrouded in illusions, but it is a powerful tool to be remembered and respected. The spiritual self contains the ego, but extends beyond it. The world it sees is wondrous and intimate. This is the beginning of building a relationship with power beyond. As the spiritual self becomes more and more the seat of awareness it extends and the sum of awareness extends with it. This creates awareness of other layers of self that extend without boundary to the edge of power beyond. Experience at this level is changed from ego level experience and it does not conform to the concepts or tools of communication used at the ego level. It is pure experience born of pure need. From this vantage point comes the understanding that much of what we thought should change is simply part of the process of the beauty and unfolding of life. As embodied by many past sages, the greater the level of awareness, the less outward change is required.

We will always spend much of our earthly time involved in the lovely experience of life with all its turmoil, emotion, and detail. But, this extended level of consciousness during envisioning is possible for human awareness to attain. It is a level within each of us. It is a level of great power and of great reverence for what is. No greed or worry, no concerns of the moment penetrate to this level. Yet when we experience it, and experience our pure need, all the levels of our being are affected. All levels are thus informed and re-formed each time. Reaching for this level is a rebalancing of all that is in our lives. Envisioning radiates from this extended level where the concerns of the ego are most distant. At this level, we are infused with the pure need of our creator and our role is clear. Our purpose flows through us into the world with complete acceptance. From the vantage point and posture of consciousness in pure experience, in acceptance of pure need, we can finally turn our attention downstream, to earthly awareness, without judgment. From within the flow of creative energy all things are possible. From there, if pure need is sensed, we can begin to influence the flow. It becomes only a matter of choosing.

To become conscious in envisioning is finally to understand free will.

Epilogue

Beyond here consider 'structures of thought' as invention.
At first we will barely be able to perceive them.
Soon, they will be manifest aspects of our lives.

About The Author

Dr. Munson has been a practicing emergency physician in Chelsea Michigan since 1983. He was board certified in emergency medicine in 1996 and 1006. Something of a non-conformist he has spent his entire carrier in the same community hospital seeing and assisting its growth from a sleepy four bed emergency room to its current busy 12 bed size. He has been a designer of three expansions and loves the creation of efficient systems within the chaotic environment of emergency medicine.

The subject of envisioning came into the Dr's life in 1989 during study with Tom Brown Jr. who is known for his many books and his school Tracker inc. that is perhaps the country's foremost wilderness survival and awareness school. Dr. Munson has been a student or participated in over eighteen classes or events at Tracker and this remains an active are of personal growth and study. Dr. Munson began teaching himself through Wild Heart, which he founded in 1993. Classes range from wilderness excursions, animal tracking to guided meditation leading toward the expansion of personal spiritual awareness.

In 2003 Dr. Munson began private practice in his hometown of Dexter Michigan in order to continue to explore the nature and function of envisioning in the healing field. Though the emergency department had proven to be an excellent arena for experimentation in personal envisioning a different environment was needed to help patients come into realization of their own envisioning. Envision Health is currently visible on the web at www.envisionhealth.org

In the future Dr. Munson is working toward offering weeklong wilderness based seminars in personal health, the expansion of awareness and the growth of personal capability.

Dr. Munson has a son and daughter who, happily, remain in Michigan as of 2007.